How to Taste
a guide to enjoying wine

How to Taste
a guide to enjoying wine

Jancis Robinson
Special photography by Jan Baldwin

Simon & Schuster
New York London Toronto Sydney Singapore

In loving memory of T. E. R.

SIMON & SCHUSTER
Rockefeller Center
1230 Avenue of the Americas
New York, NY 10020

First published as *Masterglass* in 1983
This revised edition originally published in Great Britain in
2000 by Conran Octopus Limited as *Jancis Robinson's Wine
Tasting Workbook*

SIMON & SCHUSTER and colophon are registered trademarks of
Simon & Schuster, Inc.

Manufactured in China

10 9 8 7 6 5 4 3 2 1

Library of Congress Cataloging-in-Publication Data
Robinson, Jancis
    How to taste: a guide to enjoying wine / Jancis Robinson;
special photography by Jan Baldwin.
        p. cm.
    First published as Masterglass in 1983—T.p. verso.
    Originally published: Jancis Robinson's Wine tasting
    workbook. Great Britain : Conran Octopus Limited.,
    2000— T.p. verso.
    Includes index.
    1. Wine tasting. I.Baldwin, Jan. ill. II. Title.

TP548.5.A5 R57 2001
641.2'2—dc21

                                                        2001020302

ISBN 0-7432-1677-6

Contents

Foretaste:
a book for the thirsty

This is a book for people who want to know more about wine, but have quite understandably realized that drinking wine is a lot more fun than reading about it. Happily, the practical side of wine appreciation not only has more immediate appeal than the arid theory, it is also considerably more important.

It's horribly easy for those of us who earn our living writing and talking about wine to lose sight of the fact that what actually counts is how it tastes. The lovely liquid exists not to fill analysis books or justify vintage charts, but to give sensual pleasure. This "wet" guide to wine is merely an accompaniment to your wine drinking, explaining why different wines taste the way they do, so that by being an informed wine taster (as opposed to an ignorant drinker) you can maximize your enjoyment.

This wine tasting workbook constitutes a complete wine course for the thirsty. It tells the story of how wine is made, explains how factors as diverse as climate and bottle size influence the resultant taste, and demonstrates how to get as much pleasure from wine as possible by the practical way you serve and drink it. All this information is offered here not just with words, but reinforced by scores of practical exercises—most involving that important sport, wine tasting. Each chapter is divided into theory and practice sections, so you can first absorb the relevant information and then test it yourself. (Other things you'll be asked to do range from tasting toothpaste to drinking wine from a teacup.)

The course begins with an outline of our personal tasting mechanism and highlights some surprising facts which may well help you get more out of everything you taste—food as well as wine. This is followed by a detailed look at the practical aspects of serving and drinking wine. However, the main body of the book is the story of wine told by the painless method of tasting it.

The exercises in the practical sections are meant to equip the interested wine drinker with the important explanations of why each wine tastes the way it does. Every taste-shaping factor is illustrated with specific examples, and everyone who completes the exercises should have an extremely good grasp of the fundamentals of wine in its most relevant, but often overlooked, context—in your glass. You

can literally taste your way to wine expertise. Halfway through the course, you should find that you are able to tell a Chardonnay from a Sauvignon and, by the end, a Médoc from a Coonawarra; making mistakes no more often than the wine professional—that is, no more than half the time.

There are all sorts of different factors that influence the flavor of a wine, from what goes on fifteen feet below the vineyard to whether the cellar door was left open when the wine was bottled. But the single most important and recognizable factor is the predominant grape variety that is used in the wine. For this reason, and because so many of the world's wines are now labeled as varietals (Cabernet Sauvignon, Merlot, Pinot Noir, Chardonnay, Riesling, etc.), the main part of the book is divided into sections on each of the major grape varieties.

Initially, this is simply to establish each variety's identity on the palate. A Marlborough Sauvignon from New Zealand and a Sancerre, for instance, are examples of the same grape variety, and tasting each (plus a dry white Bordeaux and a Fumé Blanc from California) will help form a "palate picture" of the Sauvignon Blanc grape. Grafted on to each section, however, is a set of increasingly complex and interrelated factors. After you've established what Sauvignon tastes like, for example, you are encouraged to taste examples made in very different climates, so that you can see how 50 percent more sunshine in a bottle actually tastes.

First of all, we look at the grapes that make "white" wines, then those that make red wines. There follows a guide to tasting sparkling and strong or "fortified" wines such as sherry and port. At the end of the book there are also some demonstrations of why some wine and food combinations don't work (though no dogma about which do), some suggestions for further wine tasting exercises, and a short glossary of the jargon used in wine tasting.

How to use this guide

If you want to learn about wine in the speediest and most systematic way that this book can offer, try to follow the exercises in the order suggested in this course, as this constitutes a logical and precise way of building up your knowledge. There's no reason, however, why you should allow me to dictate your wine-drinking habits. You could perfectly easily allow the wine you happen to be drinking to dictate the order in which you tackle this book. Simply look up the wine you are tasting in the index, which starts on page 205, and find out which exercise(s) could be useful.

Certainly, chapters 3 and 4, on white and red wines respectively, can be tackled in tandem, though even the most free-range wine taster is advised to look first at the two chapters on "Learning to taste" and "Practical matters."

You can learn a great deal by studying only one wine but, as you will see in this book, you can learn at least five times as much by tasting two and comparing them. This means that you could accelerate your progress through this course by getting together with others also interested in finding out more about wine, or by learning how to cope with wine leftovers, or by dramatically increasing your wine consumption. You, your liver, and your bank balance will determine which of the two latter possibilities is more sensible, but if you choose the first, bear in mind that a normal 75cl bottle can supply either six good glasses of wine for drinking or up to twenty samples for tasting.

In each practical exercise, examples of wines suitable for tasting have been described as specifically as is both necessary and possible. Many of them are widely available and, where possible, not too expensive. It is true, however, that in some cases, the less you are prepared to spend per bottle, the more slowly you will learn. The cheapest California Chardonnay, for example, will not express the essential characteristics of California and Chardonnay nearly as well as one that costs four or five times as much.

If you really get hooked, you may also want to try some of the more advanced exercises, which, if done with enthusiasm and at least part of your brain as well as your mouth, will turn you into a seriously well-informed wine taster.

Why you can be a great wine taster

No matter how little you know about wine now, you can learn how to taste wine by following this course. It's designed for everyone from the complete novice (nay, teetotaller) upward. I learned a great deal myself while compiling it, so I hope that others, who have been exposed to wine for some years, may do so, too—especially from chapters 1 and 2. Those who are relatively new to wine should feel particularly confident, though, since it is they who invariably make the most acute tasters.

The average adult can detect well over one thousand different flavors, many of which can be found in wine, so your tasting mechanism is already well equipped to deal with the raw material. All you need is the sort of guidance this course can offer, and some confidence. There is no such thing as a born taster. Only a tiny proportion of people whose physical disabilities have impaired their sense of taste will find any difficulty at all; and in blind tasting (tasting to identify an unnamed wine) novices often do better, because their perceptions are unclouded by previous experiences.

This course should turn you into an accomplished "blind" taster (one who can identify wines without any clues other than what they taste) but, perhaps more importantly, will show you how to assess the quality of the wine and how to get the most from it.

Despite what some self-styled "connoisseurs" may suggest, there are no rights or wrongs in wine appreciation. Tasting is in its essence a subjective business. There are some bottles which may, on an objective basis, be technically faulty, but which some tasters may find perfectly enjoyable. There are other famous wines that can count on enough admirers always to command a high price—that most quantifiable of wine measurements—yet they may not appeal at all to all wine drinkers. Never feel that you "ought" to like or dislike a wine. The most important aspect of any wine is that you enjoy it. The aim of this book is to help you enjoy wine more.

1. Learning to taste

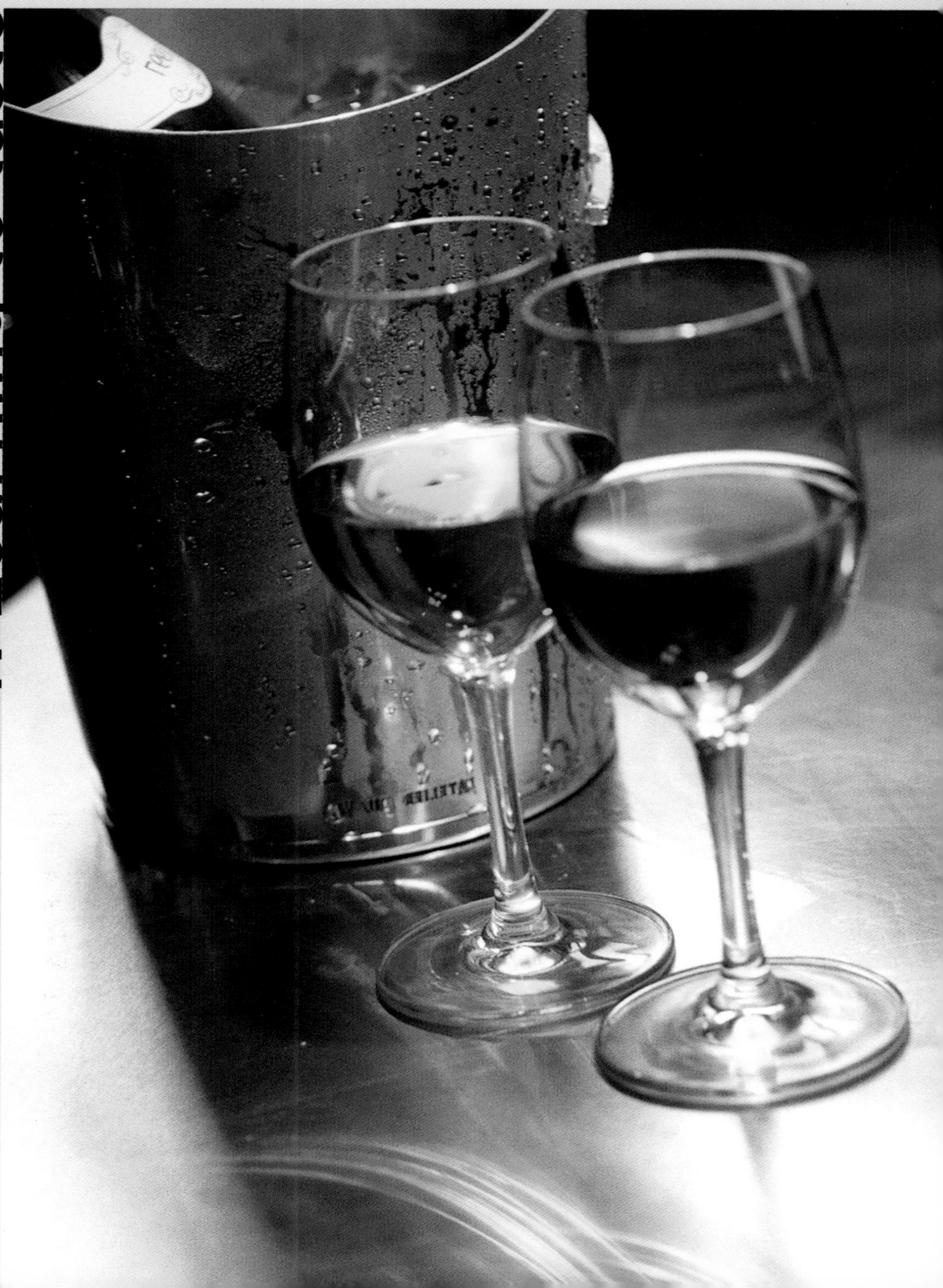

How little we know

It's extraordinary how little we know about something we do as often as eating and drinking. Once food and drink enter our digestive systems there are so many things that can go wrong that the medical profession knows a great deal about what goes on there. But surprisingly little is known about the process of tasting that precedes all of that, even though we should, in theory, be much more consciously involved in it than in the digestive process.

Few medical researchers have thought it necessary to look very carefully at how we taste, presumably because a malfunctioning gustatory system is not seen as a particularly serious affliction (though it would drive me crazy). And if the professionals know remarkably little about how the gustatory system operates in its complex role between mind and body, then we ordinary eaters and drinkers understand even less about how to get the most out of the tasting experience. Even those who would claim to appreciate the pleasures of the table have no clear idea how and why they do so. Whether you like chocolate cake, smoked salmon, or Merlot, your general approach will be to ram as much of it as possible into your digestive system (and therefore past your gustatory system) as fast as you possibly can. You are vaguely aware that by chewing the food you can prolong the pleasure it gives you, and that with wine there is some rather unsavory gargling business indulged in by professionals. But that, for most of us, constitutes our knowledge of this daily activity.

We may not know much about it, but, as so many of us proudly proclaim, we sure do know what we like. Or do we? We reckon it is the taste of food and drink that we recognize and base our judgments on, but experience shows that when we are left without any clues other than our own sense of taste we can be pretty helpless. By examining carefully how it is that we taste, this wine course should leave the reader considerably better equipped to appreciate wine—and food, for we taste solids and liquids in almost the same way; in fact, physiologically, we can't taste solids until we have transformed them into liquids by chewing them. Experiments show that it isn't possible for us to taste totally dry foods at all, so a well-blotted tongue would have no chance of telling even that sugar was sweet.

You will need a very cooperative accomplice: either someone who also wants to follow the course and on whom the tables can be turned after you have performed, or someone who loves you a lot and is prepared to indulge this latest idiosyncrasy of yours.

Familiar food

Blindfold yourself and get them to offer you a food that you like, together with one that is similar but slightly different, to see whether or not you can distinguish between them without visual clues. For example: chocolate cake and plain sponge cake; smoked salmon and smoked mackerel. (Of course they will have to be presented in the same way. If the chocolate has butter icing, then so should the plain sponge cake; and the smoked mackerel should be sliced in the same way as the smoked salmon.)

Red and white wine

Now if you thought that exercise would be easy, you'll think this next one is a cinch. But you'll probably be surprised at how difficult it is in practice to distinguish between a red and a white wine, with you still blindfolded and the wines served at the same temperature. (By the way, a pair of dark glasses can do the job of the blindfold less conspicuously.)

The odds can be weighted. Whites that taste very "red" are full bodied and dry. White Burgundy, Chardonnays, Sémillons, and some of the more traditional white Riojas are obvious examples. Reds that taste "white" have lots of acidity and not too much weight in the mouth. Pinot Noirs and Beaujolais are good candidates, as are many northeast Italian reds such as Valpolicella, and the reds of the Loire valley in northern France, Chinon, and Bourgueil.

If you want to make things easy for yourself, try to tell the difference between a light, sweetish white such as a Mosel and a full-bodied, none-too-acid red such as one from Argentina, Barossa Valley, or Châteauneuf-du-Pape. Even then, you will probably be surprised to find you have to think twice before pronouncing. And if you try the experiment simply on the most basic, cheapest red and white, the house wines in your local for example, you'll probably have to think very hard indeed.

The importance of the nose

We tend to think that just as food and drink have a "look" that is registered by the eyes, they have a "smell" that is detected by the nose, and a "taste" that is sensed by the mouth. In fact, the line of distinction between the second two is very blurred.

If you have a cold and your nose is blocked up, just think how little taste everything seems to have. When you smell something cooking in the oven, don't you feel as though you already know how it's going to taste? If you want to judge whether you would enjoy the taste of a soup someone is offering you, you smell it.

What we call the "taste" of something is actually the composite impression it makes on our minds by what we sense through our noses and our mouths. But, as suggested above, our noses are in fact more sensitive than our mouths. Without our sense of smell we are unable to appreciate foods or distinguish between them easily. "Flavor" is a less misleading term than "taste," which we tend to think of as connected with our mouths.

There are two aspects of a substance that can carry a message to our brains: what is tangible, the liquid or solid that comes into contact with our tongue and the inside of our mouth, and what is vaporized, the usually invisible gas that is given off by the substance. When we're consciously smelling something, whether a wine, a food, or a shampoo, it's this vapor that travels up our nose to the olfactory receptors at the top. When we're chewing the same thing, the vapor travels from the back of our mouths, up what's called the retro-nasal passage, to the same sensory organ. So what we think of as "tasting" actually includes quite a bit of unconscious "smelling," and what we call the "taste" of something necessarily includes a bit of the "smell."

Although it is difficult for us to do controlled experiments because we can't shut off the retro-nasal passage, it seems fairly certain that the messages that solids and liquids are able to convey are much less subtle than those wafted up in vapor. This is because our sensing equipment for vapor is capable of much finer distinctions than that for solids and liquids—the tongue and inside of the mouth. By cutting off our sense of smell as much as possible and simply chewing, we are left with a much less complex impression of the flavor of something than if we don't have it in our mouths at all, but simply smell it—provided, of course, that it's the sort of substance that does give off some sort of vapor.

Different substances vary tremendously in the amount of vapor they have to give. If they are very volatile and have lots of little flavor elements shooting off into the atmosphere all the time, then smelling them will be an interesting and rewarding experience. Wine is very volatile compared, say, to its biblical partner, bread. You don't get nearly as much vapor from a slice of bread as from a glass of wine—though there is a lot of vapor from freshly baked bread straight out of the oven, because the heat has encouraged all the flavor elements to vaporize. Think how much more flavor soup seems to have when it is hot than when it has been allowed to cool. A bowl of cooled soup is not very volatile and therefore not very appetizing, whereas a bowl of hot, volatile soup can be wonderfully enticing, because of the intriguing mesh of messages carried to your olfactory receptors by the vapor. The messages that are conveyed to the brain by the nose are not necessarily stronger than those messages that are conveyed by the mouth, but they are more subtle. Wine is one of the most subtle substances we will ever taste, and one that is naturally volatile and doesn't need to be heated up to give off a vapor full of flavor. It makes sense therefore to smell a wine every time you drink it.

BY ACTIVELY SMELLING EVERYTHING YOU DRINK (AND EAT) YOU CAN AT LEAST DOUBLE THE PLEASURE IT GIVES.

Holding your nose

Next time you eat, try tasting a mouthful with your nose pinched tight shut. Notice how much the flavor of the food changes. If your mouth is shut as well, the food is left in a chamber that is enclosed except for the passage at the back of the mouth—and it starts to taste much cruder. A bit of pineapple, for instance, tastes like something that is juicy, sweet, and tart, but without the distinctive pineapple-ness that the nose usually picks up. A spoonful of soup tastes wet and a bit salty, but the flavor isn't nearly as intense as it is when allowed to steam up your nostrils.

Get someone (who will promise not to laugh) to blindfold you and put some sort of nose-clamp on you, whether it be fingers, a clothespin, a bulldog clip, or a swimmer's noseclip. Choose three similarly textured but differently flavored foods, such as grated apple, potato, and carrot, and see whether you can distinguish between a mouthful of each. If you fail, try adding a really obvious one like grated onion just to boost your confidence. But don't despair if even the bulb eludes you; it has baffled physiologists' human guinea pigs before.

Tasting the vapor

When not actually ingesting, do keep your mouth closed during the two experiments outlined above. If you draw in air over the food you're chewing, it will encourage the vapor given off to travel up the retro-nasal passage and give the same sort of messages as the nose would. Notice, too, that as you chew, you break the food down into a mush that you move toward the back of your mouth. It is from there, if your nostrils aren't blocked, that you "sniff up" the vapor to the olfactory center.

Inside the mouth

Basic granulated sugar is not very volatile. Take a sniff of the sugar bowl. You get a sort of "flat" smell at best, but even that is straining the imagination. Basically, sugar doesn't smell. It has no easily discernible effect on your nostrils, but it will have a major impact on your (unblotted!) tongue and the inside of your mouth once you have a spoonful of it in there. This is nothing subtle. No great nuances of flavor here, but a coating of the tongue with a great wham of what you know as "sweetness," particularly on the tip of the tongue, and a sort of grating brought about by its coarse, grainy texture. These sensations are a good example of the two possible ways a food or drink can have an impact on us when inside the mouth: respectively by taste or by texture. We look at texture later.

WARMING A WINE ENCOURAGES IT TO GIVE OFF MORE VAPOR, MAKING IT MORE "SMELLY."

More detail is given at the end of this chapter about the crucial business of wine smelling (so important it has been graced with the dignified title "nosing"), but it is useful first to see how much information you can get from your mouth. As demonstrated by the sugar exercise on page 15, we get very strong sensations from our tongue. Almost all of what we call our taste buds (and the amount we have ranges enormously from five hundred to ten thousand) are located on the tongue, each of them particularly well tuned to one of the basic elements of taste. Physiologists have identified at least four—sweetness, sourness, saltiness, and bitterness—and argue about others, which might include oiliness, alkalinity, fattiness, "metallic-ness," and something called "umami" of which monosodium glutamate is a prime example. The first four comprise a very useful model, and different areas of the tongue are supposed to be particularly sensitive to each of them. Of course, individuals vary in their own sensitivities, and you will be able to identify exactly where on your tongue you are most sensitive to each. It is therefore important to use as much of your tongue as possible with everything you taste. To paraphrase: take a good mouthful.

Sweetness in wine

In very general terms, the highest concentration of those taste buds that are particularly aware of sweetness is around the tip of the tongue. Perhaps this is why we need only a tiny lick of ice cream to know how sweet it is, and why a single lick of a chocolate can convey so much more than a single lick of cheese, for example.

Grape juice becomes wine when yeasts act on the sugar in ripe grapes to convert some, or nearly all, of it (in a way too complicated for most of us to even contemplate) into alcohol. The resulting liquid is therefore drier and stronger than grape juice, but the amount of sweetness left in the finished wine—the "residual sugar"—varies enormously. Wine can be extra dry, dry, medium dry, medium sweet, sweet, or very sweet; though even wines we normally label "bone dry," because they seem to have no sweetness at all, contain a tiny amount of residual sugar. Sugar content ranges from about .035 to more than 7 ounces per quart, with dry wines usually containing less than 0.38 ounces and often as few as 0.07. Most very cheap wines and many very popular ones have quite a lot of residual sugar because, respectively, sweetness can mask many a rough edge and it is a very easy taste to appreciate.

In recent years, however, the mass market has been schooled to feel proud of liking something dry, though now there are instances of inverse snobbery in people such as myself, who perhaps make a bit more noise about liking German wines and Sauternes than we would if they were more generally appreciated.

Tasting the sweetness

Experiment with sugar granules to see where on your tongue you experience sweetness best. Then whenever you drink a liquid, try to assess its sweetness by its impact on your tongue. Now try the same procedure with every wine that comes your way, taking conscious note of the amount of sweetness you detect in every wine you drink. Notice, again with the sugar bowl, that you can't actually smell sugar. There are all sorts of flavors associated with sweetness—ripe fruit flavors and vanilla, for example—but the nose alone cannot measure sugar levels.

Levels of sweetness in white wine

Bone dry
Muscadet; Loire wines based on the Sauvignon grape such as Sancerre, Pouilly-Fumé, and Sauvignon de Touraine; most champagne and other sparkling wines labelled "brut"; proper Chablis from northern France; Germany's "trocken" wines.

Dry
(The biggest category, though within it there are variations, with cheaper versions tending towards medium dry): Most Chardonnay, Sauvignon Blanc, Sémillon, Verdelho, Colombard; white Burgundy; Loire wines labeled "sec" and based on the Chenin Blanc grape, such as Vouvray and Saumur; white Rhône and Provence wines such as Hermitage Blanc or Châteauneuf-du-Pape Blanc; most white Bordeaux labeled "sec"; most white "vin de pays"; Soave, Verdicchio, Pinot Grigio, Pinot Bianco, and most white "vino da tavola"; white Rioja; Germany's "halbtrocken" wines and some of its lightest "Kabinett" wines; Fino and Manzanilla sherry.

Medium dry
Riesling, Viognier, Gewürztraminer, Chenin Blanc, Pinot Gris; most French wines labeled "demi sec", especially Vouvrays, and Coteaux du Layon; most Alsace wines; Frascati; the majority of German wine exported and certainly those labeled Kabinett, Spätlese, or Halbtrocken; Dry Amontillado or Dry Oloroso sherry; white port.

Medium sweet
Most wines labeled Late Harvest; most French wines labeled "moelleux"; "vendange tardive" wines from Alsace; Asti, and most Moscato; Moscatel de Setúbal; Tokay from Hungary; German Auslese and Mosel Beerenauslese; most white Zinfandel and other blush wines; commercial Amontillado sherry; most madeira.

Sweet
Most wines labeled "botrytized" or "Selected Late Harvest"; Sauternes, Barsac, Monbazillac, Saussignac, Ste. Croix du Mont; French Muscats; German Trockenbeerenauslese; most Recioto and Passito; Vin Santo; California Muscat; commercial Oloroso sherry; Malmsey madeira.

Very sweet
Spanish Moscatel; Australian Liqueur Muscat and Tokay; Cream and Pedro Ximénez sherry; a host of fortified wines.

Sweet red wine

We tend to think that it's only white wines that vary in sweetness. Rosés do as well, of course, with Provence making generally quite dry ones, while Mateus Rosé is an example of wine that is medium dry to medium sweet. But it is perhaps more of a revelation to examine the varying degrees of sweetness in red wines. Port is the supreme example of a very sweet red, but it is a wine that has been fortified by the addition of extra alcohol (see Chapter 5 for more on fortified wines).

Try some of the red wines listed below to see how much sweetness can vary in red wines, though admittedly most reds can be described as "dry."

Levels of sweetness in red wine

Bone dry
Red Loires such as Bourgueil, Chinon, and Saumur Rouge; typical Médoc and Pessac-Léognan; Hermitage; Italy's great reds such as Barolo, Barbaresco, Brunello di Montalcino, and Chianti Classico.

Dry
About 85 percent of all reds.

Medium dry
Most varietal Merlot and Pinot Noir; some California Cabernet Sauvignon, much Zinfandel; Châteauneuf-du-Pape; Lambrusco; Freisa; most German reds; Australian Shiraz; South Africa's beefier reds; most inexpensive branded reds.

Medium sweet
Sangria; sparkling Shiraz; Recioto della Valpolicella; most Brachetto; California's late-harvest Zinfandels.

Acidity—the vital spark

Sweetness (or lack of it, i.e. dryness) may be the most obvious of the four basic tastes to students of wine, but what physiologists call sourness is the most vital to the wine itself.

Sourness is a measure of acidity, of which there's a lot in lemon juice and vinegar and little or none in flour and water. The upper edges of the tongue (toward the back of the mouth for me) are most sensitive to acidity.

Too much acidity makes something sour; just enough enlivens it, giving it an appealing "zip" or a crisp tartness. Sweetness and acidity are closely interrelated. As a fruit ripens, it gets sweeter and sweeter while losing acidity. An over-ripe pear, for instance, is bland and unappetizing because it has so much less acidity than one picked at just the right moment.

Getting the balance between sweetness and acidity right in wine grapes is crucial. The winemaker wants his grapes to be as ripe as possible for two reasons. Firstly, the longer the grapes are on the vine the more interesting flavors they will have had time to develop; and, secondly, the sweeter the grape juice the sweeter and/or stronger the resultant wine will be, strength being seen as a tantalizing commodity in wine regions far from the Equator. The wine producer must not, on the other hand, leave the grapes on the vine so long that the acidity falls to a level that will make the wine bland (or so long that they will be ruined by rain, hail, or frost). And, for white wines designed to live long, acidity acts as a sort of embalming fluid.

There are many different acids in wine, the most common being tartaric; indeed, scrapings from the insides of used wine vats are the chief ingredient in commercially available "cream of tartar" preparations. Embryonic wine tasters need not worry if you are unable to distinguish between, say, gluconic and glyconic acids; all you need be concerned about is the general level of acidity as it appears to your senses. The acidity level may be high for several reasons: the wine was made from grapes grown where ripening sunshine has been at a premium (either because of distance from the Equator or altitude of the vineyard); the grapes were picked before they were fully ripe; there was not enough sunshine in that year to ripen the grapes fully; or acidity has been deliberately added to the wine or must (the fermenting grape juice). This is common practice in warmer wine regions and, when done carefully and undetectably to the taster, can often make for a better end-result.

Pure acid

Take a sniff of something that is high in acidity. Vinegar of any sort is fine (lemon juice is not as volatile). Notice how the edges of your tongue curl up in anticipation of the experience of how it is going to taste in your mouth. Acidity has such a strong effect on the tongue that it is the easiest of the four basic tastes to imagine without any liquid or solid stimulus at all. But if you really want to prove this point to yourself, try sipping some lemon juice or vinegar. Whether imagining, smelling, or sipping, notice which part of your tongue reacts most strongly to acidity.

Acidity and sweetness

Now start smelling every drink you take, whether it's alcoholic or not. Notice that most drinks do actually have some sort of refreshing acidity in them. Still water won't make your tongue crinkle—it marks the frontier between acid and alkaline—but all fruit juices, carbonated drinks, milk, and even tea and coffee have some sort of tingling effect on the tongue. Notice too how important a component acidity is in fruit; lemons, grapefruit, gooseberries, and blackcurrants are all common

examples of fruits with so much natural acid that most of us have to add extra sweetness before we can eat them. Monitor the different tastes in a batch of fast-ripening fruits, such as pears or tomatoes, as they lose their natural acidity and start to taste dull. Start registering acid levels as you taste wine.

If you have some cream of tartar in the house, make up a solution of it and add it in varying amounts to an ordinary table wine, maybe one of those cheap, bland whites that are exported in such quantity from Germany. (Heaven forbid such desecration of anything smart.) You might even be able to "correct" it to a more acceptable level of acidity.

Acid test

To get a very, very crude idea of the flavors of different sorts of acidity found in wine, familiarize yourself with these:

tartaric acid—cream of tartar in solution

malic acid—apple juice

citric acid—lemons, grapefruit, or orange juice

lactic acid—milk or yogurt

acetic acid—vinegar

carbonic acid—fizzy drinks

Balancing sweetness and acidity

The delicate balance between sweetness and acidity in ripe grapes is reflected in the resulting wines. The sweeter the wine, the more acidity is needed to stop it being cloying. The most obvious difference between a poor and a great Sauternes is the amount of acidity there is to counterbalance all that sugar.

At the other end of the spectrum, a very dry wine doesn't need all that much acidity to make it taste appetizing and crisp. A bone-dry wine that had as much acidity as a Sauternes would be mouth-puckeringly tart. The acidity of wine tends to range between .105 and .315 ounces of tartaric acid per quart.

Getting the balance between sugar and acidity right is an important part of winemaking. Wines that are too high in acidity right from the start are called green. There is nothing sacred or technical about the term "green," of course; it just happens to be an adjective commonly used for over-acid wines. "Tart" is another word used for the phenomenon, though more often for whites than reds. Noticeable but not overwhelming acidity is a very desirable quality in white wines, for we expect them to refresh us, whereas most red wines are expected to provide more nourishment and a bit of intrigue. Whites with marked, but not unpleasant, acidity are often called "crisp." Wines, both red and white, that have rather too little acidity are often called "flabby," one of those words that gives wine tasters a bad name. Yes, it does sound a bit ridiculous. If you can't bear to use it, you could use "flat" instead. A flat or flabby wine is merely dull because it lacks sufficient acidity to enliven it. A cloying wine is one that is really sweet and does not contain enough acidity to balance the sweetness.

It can be devilishly easy to confuse acidity and dryness. A lot of us think we're drinking a very dry wine because it seems like hard work, when in fact it may simply be too high in acidity. Because a little sweetness is useful to mask none-too-brilliant winemaking, it's a favorite trick of the blenders of cheap "dry" whites to market a medium-dry wine with a massive dollop of acid in it to keep the fans happy. And those trying to make balanced wines in regions whose wines are naturally high in acidity may add a bit of unfermented grape juice to sweeten the final blend, counterbalancing the acidity.

SHAKE OFF THAT ANTI-SWEET WINE PREJUDICE!

A good balance

Treat yourself to a good Sauternes, which in general means a classed growth with *cru classé* on the label. Half bottles are common, and in a good one, the high sugar content will be appetizingly counterbalanced by a high level of acidity so it won't be at all cloying and you can sip it on its own, or with a not-too-sweet dessert, or cheese. Compare it with a really inexpensive sweet white Bordeaux or Monbazillac. Notice how much sicklier and less refreshing the cheaper wine is because it does not have sufficient acidity.

Try a Loire white labeled "sec." Notice how acid it seems to taste, because this northerly region's naturally high level of acidity is not counterbalanced by any appreciable sweetness.

Taste an inexpensive white Vin de Pays des Côtes de Gascogne. It is obviously high in acidity, but look behind that to notice just how much sweetness has been left in it to counterbalance that.

Start registering acidity levels as you taste wine. The table on the following page lists some possible examples of wines at each end of the spectrum.

Levels of acidity

Green or tart

Gros Plant Nantais from the Loire; Coteaux Champenois (the still wines of
Champagne; I always think they demonstrate perfectly why champagne should have
bubbles in it); many English wines; Luxembourg's wines; many 1996 Burgundies (of
either color); Vinho Verde from Portugal.

Crisp

Most New Zealand wines; almost all Loire wines, no matter how sweet they are;
Mosel wines; Chablis and lots of other white Burgundy; lots of other well-made
whites from slightly warmer regions.

Flabby or flat

Much more difficult to generalize here as it depends on individual winemakers' skills,
but southern Rhône, North African, and other wines made close to Mediterranean
shores tend to flab (including old-fashioned Spanish wines such as Monastrell). You
will sense a sort of drabness in the overall impact of the wine and find yourself still
looking for the refreshment that would have been provided by a bit of acidity as the
wine goes through the mouth.

Cloying or too sweet

Cheap, very sweet wines of all sorts, either sweet white Bordeaux such as poor
quality Sauternes or Barsac or the sweetest representatives in a range of branded
wines. Now try the "dry white" in such a range—perhaps a glass of dry white at your
local pub—and see if, by carefully registering how your tongue reacts, you can sort
out the sweetness from the acidity.

BURGUNDY—WHOSE WHITE
WINES ARE CHARDONNAY,
WHICH ARE ALMOST
INVARIABLY DRY.

The other basic tastes

Salt

Saltiness is a basic taste that is vitally important in food but rarely found in wine. Dry sherry of any hue can be slightly salty, and I sometimes taste a trace of saltiness in Chilean reds, New Zealand whites, and many Syrahs from the northern Rhône such as Hermitage and Crozes-Hermitage, but such perceptible saline intrusions into the world of wine are exceptional. The description of the salt-tasting mechanism is included here more for completeness than for usefulness in wine tasting.

Make up a saline solution by dissolving some salt in water and swill it about your mouth, noticing which parts of the tongue react most strongly. I find it is the part just in from the ultra-acid-conscious edges at the back, and bits of the front edges, too. Next time you want to check the seasoning in some savory dish, make sure this part of your tongue is exposed to your sample of it.

Next time you smell or taste a Fino or Manzanilla sherry—the very dry, light ones, Tio Pepe and La Ina are good examples—notice how the salt-sensitive parts of your tongue react to their taste.

ALL SHERRY IS MATURED IN OLD OAK "BUTTS."

Bitterness

This is the fourth and final basic taste that the tongue is capable of registering, and which the flat back part of the tongue is particularly sensitive to. Like saltiness, bitterness is much less important to wine tasters than sweetness and acidity, but quite a number of Italian reds leave a bitter taste at the back of the tongue. (Bitterness is often confused with tannin, but you will see how it affects a quite different part of your mouth.)

To isolate bitterness, you could try putting a few drops of bitters such as Fernet Branca, Underberg, Angostura, or Suze in some water and rinsing that around your mouth. You will notice a flat, rasping sensation on the back part of your tongue. Campari is another very bitter liquid, but it is also very sweet—an interesting tasting exercise in itself. See how it needs the acidity of soda water (carbonic acid) and/or a slice of lemon or orange (citric acid) to make it a refreshing drink. The Italians obviously have a certain monopoly on bitterness (they adore drinks described as "amari" or bitter). Assess each Italian red you taste for bitterness. Some Chianti and some of the most renowned Brunello di Montalcino, Vino Nobile di Montepulciano, Barolo, and Barbaresco have some degree of bitterness, as do many examples of the generally lighter and fruitier Valpolicella. So long as it is not present in excess, bitterness need not be a fault; in fact some medical authorities recommend bitters for their ability to aid digestion and help the body cope with alcohol.

THE SEAL OF THE CHIANTI CLASSICO CONSORZIO.

So now your tongue should be fully trained to do its damnedest with any wine (and, more important, food) that comes its way. You should be able to assess the sweetness and acidity of any substance—as well as its saltiness and bitterness if necessary. You may be glad to hear that you now have a scientific excuse to take your wine in fairly large mouthfuls, for you should expose all of your tongue to the liquid.

Of course, you won't always carefully identify each basic taste separately. The wine makes a composite impression on your senses as you swill it about your mouth, but sweetness and acidity are crucial to that overall impression.

More crude feelings

You can learn a bit more than the simple sensations of sweetness, acidity, saltiness, and bitterness from the tangible effect of a wine on your tongue and the insides of your mouth.

One of the most obvious, and sometimes even pain-inducing ingredients in many red wines is tannin. This is a convenient shorthand term for all sorts of tannins or polyphenols that either find their way into a wine from the pips (that is, the seeds), grape skins, and stems, or develop as a result of the wood in which the wine has been stored—or sometimes both.

Tannin

In ordinary eating and drinking, tannin is most noticeable in tea, particularly when it has been allowed to stand and lots of tannin has been extracted from the leaves. (That thin skin on walnuts is also a good example.) The sensation that tannin produces in the mouth is perhaps even more crude than any we have studied so far. The insides of the mouth and the gums seem to pucker up in a pretty nasty way when confronted by noticeable tannin (they are literally being tanned, like leather): one reason why tasting young red wines that are destined for great things can be hard work.

Maturing with age

Wines don't contain tannin to taste good now, but in the hope that they will taste good in the future. Just as white wines designed to be kept need acidity in their youth, tannin acts as a sort of preservative to prolong the active life of a great red wine. Wine is capable of absorbing all sorts of tiny flavor elements when young, but needs time for these to knit together to produce a complex, mature wine. The tannins themselves break down and combine with other elements to contribute toward this ideal. One of the skills of the winemaker is to judge just how much tannin is needed at the beginning to balance the other flavor elements, most of them from the grape, as they evolve. Red Bordeaux and other serious Cabernet Sauvignon–dominated wines provide the best examples of this. Many vintages of these wines are capable of achieving venerable and gracious old age, which will be all the more gracious if they contain a fair amount of tannin at the outset.

THE SMALL GRAPES OF CABERNET
SAUVIGNON MEAN THERE IS ALWAYS
A HIGH PROPORTION OF SKIN, AND
THEREFORE TANNIN, TO GRAPE FLESH.

A tasting of young, good quality red Bordeaux under three years old, say, can be a great strain. The tannin content is so high that it puckers the mouth immediately, leaving the senses straining to detect some indication of fruit. Very few people are sufficiently experienced and masochistic to judge wines of this sort. "Hard" is the word used to describe a wine that has too much tannin.

One of the great preoccupations of modern red winemakers has been to make wines with softer, riper, more approachable tannins—partly by picking the grapes later and partly by treating the nascent wine more gently. The Californians have long become masters at this.

When tannin comes into its own

As the wines mature, the tannins become less evident and the taste seems much softer. The fruit-based flavors at last start to emerge in subtle and complex formations. Ideally, the tannin will fade to insignificance as the wine's flavor reaches its peak of maturity (though of course no one knows when this peak has been reached until it has passed). Part of wine's great interest is that it is so unpredictable. A vintage that can look good at the outset, so good that winemakers are happy that the wines contain lots of tannin to preserve them for a glorious future, can fail to come up with the goods, and the fruit will fade long before the tannin dissipates.

Some red wines are designed to be low in tannin, while others may be less than perfect because they have too little tannin. This doesn't make for unpleasant drinking in the way that over-tannic wines do—it's merely a waste of potential. A wine may have lots of lovely gutsy fruitiness when young, offering immediate attractive, soft drinking; but all these flavors would have been capable of maturing into something more magnificent had there been more tannin to preserve them into middle or old age.

Tea and tannin

Allow some tea to stew in the pot and then take a mouthful, without any milk to soften the impact of this ungenerous liquid. Notice how you react. There's a bit of acidity there, perhaps a trace of bitterness too, but there's also something quite different from either of these components that is so distasteful it almost makes you want to screw up your eyes. This is tannin, and I feel the puckering sensation strongest between my gums and the insides of my cheeks. Notice where it affects you most, as it will depend on how you drink. Some people notice it particularly on the roof of the mouth.

California wine

Next time you are entertaining (because this exercise will cost quite a bit), serve a young red Bordeaux, preferably a wine labeled Médoc, St. Estèphe, Pauillac, St. Julien, or Margaux, and an ambitious California or Chilean Cabernet Sauvignon of the same vintage (and about the same price). Notice how much smoother and sweeter the American wine seems, and how much less the insides of your mouth react to it than to the inkier Bordeaux.

Tannin and great wine

Now try to assess every red wine you drink for its tannic impact on your mouth. Somewhat ironically, most examples of over-tannic wines cost rather a lot because, although they are youthful, they are "fine wines" whose purpose is to be profitably cellared for many a year. For a textbook example of good wine at this early, unfriendly stage, you will have to spend quite a bit on a bottle of good 1996 Médoc (see the village names under "California wine"). Compare this with a similar wine (ideally one from the same property) from the softer 1997 vintage in which the tannins seem less obvious. And a bottle from a much older, good vintage—1990, 1989, 1985 or 1982 perhaps—would show how lovely a wine can be once the tannin has retreated into the background and allowed the fruit and oak flavors to marry and produce many different nuances.

Wines with less tannin

Tannin is not an important constituent of Beaujolais, for example, nor is it in typical Rioja (although it is noticeable in most Ribera del Duero). The wines of northeast Italy, including Merlot and Cabernet, are also soft, and even Bordeaux is producing some inexpensive low-tannin wines based on the usually tannic Cabernet Sauvignon grape. Most New World Pinot Noir is also low in tannin and, as a general rule, Merlot always tastes less tannic than Cabernet.

White wine and tannin

Tannin is chiefly an important component of red wines, partly because grape skins, stems and pips don't play an important part in white winemaking (see Chapter 3) and partly because the pigments derived from the skins are needed to interact with the tannins to soften them. Some white wines taste astringent, in the same way as tannic reds, because they have been made from grape juice that has been pressed very hard and roughly out of the grapes, so that they contain a certain amount of tannin from the skins and pips.

White wines have an astringency of their own. We tend to call whites "astringent" instead of tannic, but the feeling in the mouth is the same. Next time you taste a cheap Italian white, notice what happens to the most puckerable bit of your mouth. For me, many cheap Soaves produce the same sensation as youthful Cabernets. although the overall quality of Soave has been rising recently.

Thick-skinned grapes

Different red grape varieties tend to produce wines with different levels of tannin. The "pippier" the grapes and the thicker the skins, the higher the tannin content in the must. Cabernet Sauvignon, Syrah, and Nebbiolo grapes are particularly tannic. Vintages when there has been a shortage of rain to swell the flesh of the grapes also tend to produce tannic wines because skins and pips represent a high proportion of the must. You can taste drought.

The winemaker can try to extract as much tannin as possible from the grapes by the way he chooses to make the wine. If he encourages a long fermentation and then lets the wine rest in contact with the skins for an extended period after that, called the *cuvaison* in France, there will be ample opportunity for lots of tannin to seep out of the skins and into the wine.

When wine is left in contact with wood it tends to extract the tannin in the wood. The less an oak cask has been used, and the less it has been charred, the more tannins there are. So really great wines that are thought capable of aging up to five decades are often put into new casks. Although such casks are much more expensive than used ones, they set the wine up better for a long life.

The longer a wine is left in wood casks, the more its natural fruitiness will dissipate. Some very traditionally made Barolos are good examples of wines that have been kept so long in wood that the tannin overwhelms every other flavor component in the wine. There has been a discernible move toward making wines that are slightly softer and more approachable in Piedmont, however, just as there has been elsewhere.

Whenever a bottle of Barolo or Barbaresco from a lesser vintage (1992 or 1993, for example) comes your way, see what you think is its predominant characteristic. Typically, you will find such a Barolo so dry and so drying that drinking it without food is unthinkable. Drinking such a wine from one of the more traditional producers can be like sucking a matchstick.

Slimline and fuller-bodied wines

Just like people, wines have a weight—though there is no vinous shame in being full bodied.

A wine's weight is a measure of how much extract and alcohol it has. A full-bodied wine has an alcohol content of at least 13 percent. A light wine will probably be less than 10 percent alcohol and is a much flimsier specimen. It's difficult to describe how you assess weight, but it is actually quite easy to do. Simply by looking at the wine you can get a clue (see "A fourth twirl," page 48) and, with practice, when you smell it you often get quite a strong hint.

But it is in the mouth that wine sends its strongest "guess-the-weight" message: it really is the physical sensation of how heavy the liquid feels in the mouth. When you have a mouthful of the wine do you feel overwhelmed by the intensity of what is in there, or is it a much more watery liquid? (Water makes up well over 80 percent of the volume of most wines.) A particularly alcoholic wine leaves a hot, burning sensation once it has been swallowed (or, perish the thought, spat out).

Fortified wines are all very full bodied because they contain added alcohol. Most of the heaviest non-fortified wines are reds such as the Amarone wines of Italy, Hermitage, and Châteauneuf-du-Pape of the Rhône, late-picked Zinfandels from California, many Spanish and Argentine reds, and typical Cabernet Sauvignons from California, Australia, and South Africa. Great white Burgundy, Sauternes, and, especially, California Chardonnays can, however, be very full indeed. Significant alcohol actually tastes rather sweet, which is why so many California Chardonnays taste as though they contain more residual sugar than they actually do.

Most German wines are very light bodied; indeed, some are only about 8 percent alcohol. Vinho Verde, whether white or the rarely exported red, is also light. Beaujolais and a host of French reds such as most Vins de Pays are relatively light, even though most of us think of all reds as fairly full bodied.

A wine doesn't have to have lots of residual sugar to be full. Great Italians such as Brunello and Barolo can be full but dry, while frothy white Asti is sweet but light. If you are watching your weight, go for wines that are both light and dry. Obvious examples of these wines that are made in France are Muscadet, Sancerre, Chablis, and Beaujolais.

Alcohol content and weight

Start taking note of the alcohol content when it is stated on a wine label and relating it to how "heavy" the wine feels in your mouth. If a wine is very alcoholic, you may well feel like avoiding naked flames when you breathe out. Beware the candles after the Châteauneuf. Notice particularly the hot, alcoholic sensation you feel on your breath after swallowing port.

Light German wine

Examine a glass of Riesling from Germany, especially the Mosel, alongside one from Alsace, Austria, or Australia. Notice how much lighter the German one feels in the mouth—even though it has just as much flavor.

Dry and full; sweet and light

Try to taste a Hermitage, a Barolo or Barbaresco and notice how dry yet full bodied they are. Next time you sip some Asti or, preferably, Moscato d'Asti (which is generally superior and can be fresh, grapey, and delicious) savor its lightness at the same time as noticing how sweet it is on the tip of your tongue.

Capturing the flavor

If all a wine could tell us was that it was crisp, medium dry, fairly light, and slightly astringent, there would be no need for this book, and little pleasure in wine drinking.

Wine's great attraction is that, more than any other drink, it is capable of an amazing range of flavors—particularly when one considers that there is only one raw ingredient. (Imagine smart societies devoted to tasting different vintages of fermented carrot juice, or specialist gourmet tours of potato warehouses.)

As we have seen, our taste buds are capable of receiving only the fairly crude messages that the liquid wine can transmit. The really interesting bit, the wine's character that we call its flavor, is carried by the volatile elements—up through the nose when we sniff and up from the back of the mouth when we taste—to the olfactory center, the ultra-sensitive mechanism that deals with flavor. The vapor of the wine consists of the volatile molecules that form only a tiny but vital proportion of each wine's composition. It is the particular profile of these molecules that makes up each wine's flavor, and to experience this flavor fully it does, of course, make sense to get the vapor up to the olfactory center by consciously smelling or "nosing" the wine.

The words to say it

Now for the problem: how to describe wine flavor. "Mmm, delicious" or even "Urggh" will do perfectly well—if you never want to communicate with anyone else about wine, if you see no need to remember anything about specific wines, or if you choose not to enjoy the pleasures of comparison and monitoring that wine can offer. Readers of this book, however, will already have decided that they are interested in tasting wine properly, in order to assess it and to enjoy it more—possibly even with a view to blind tasting. What you will find is how frustrating it is to be confronted by a wide and thrilling range of sensations for which there is no cut-and-dried notation or vocabulary.

Music lovers know perfectly well what is meant by middle C and *fortissimo*. Connoisseurs of the visual arts agree on what is meant by square and (more or less) scarlet. For wine tasters, however, there is no objective vocabulary or measurement of something as simple and distinctive as the flavor of the Gamay grape, say; let alone for the nuances from the various other factors that paint the "palate picture," such as the soil the grapes were grown in, the weather that led up to the harvest, and the way the wine was made and stored.

Finding parallels

An accepted vocabulary would clearly be very useful for wine tasters, and considerable efforts are being made to agree on one. Each nation has their accepted tasting terms, but there is no way of extracting and comparing the sensory impression each of us associates with a given word because the business of tasting is so essentially hidden and subjective. (We each have slightly different tasting equipment and sensitivities.)

Some work has been done by an enterprising Burgundian, Jean Lenoir, to come up with definitive essences representing in a very concrete and indisputable way exactly what each term "smells" like. The Burgundian has even marketed a little box of vials under the brand name "Le Nez du Vin" so that, as you taste a wine, you can smartly refer to the essence bank to see whether you are right to describe it as "woody" or as "violets."

But there are curious disparities between different nationalities and which flavors they associate with wine. In South Africa, for example, "guava" is a common tasting note. Californians are more likely to spot "bell pepper." The more traditional French tasters go in for long lists of scents such as "acacia," "toast," "honey," and "chocolate"; while Australians are more likely to dissect a wine into component chemicals such as aldehydes and sulfides.

As most of these examples suggest, choosing words to describe wine is largely a matter of making comparisons with things that are not wine. Earlier parts of this course suggested terms such as "medium dry," "full-bodied," and "soft," which are fairly widely accepted conventions for describing some of wine's more obvious dimensions, the sorts of things that can be detected in the mouth rather than by the nose. When it comes to something as subtle as the wine's flavor, however, finding suitable descriptions is more difficult. It's a bit like the difference between describing someone's physical attributes (height, complexion, and so on) and their character. Tasters tend to look for similarities to other flavors they've experienced or can imagine.

Sometimes accepted tasting terms bear only the loosest of similarities to the flavors whose names they carry. The distinctive smell of the Gewürztraminer grape is commonly called by wine professionals "spicy." This is not because Gewürz smells like any particular spice, but because Gewürz is German for "spiced" and the tasting term "spicy" has become a convenient and accepted shorthand, or "trigger word," for the smell of Gewürz.

What works for you

You can evolve your own wine tasting vocabulary. If a wine smells like clean sheets or tennis balls to you, then register the connection. It may help you identify flavors and wines later on. All you need is a term that leads you from a sniff of the wine to recognition or a judgment of it. We all have our own trigger words for various flavors. Throughout the rest of the wine course I will try to suggest a wide range of possible terms for each flavor examined, in the hope that at least one of them will help you to develop your own tasting vocabulary. It will be useful, but not essential, if your vocabulary is like that of other people. Non-professionals can make up their own rules for the game of wine tasting—though people in the wine trade who attempt its stiffest test, the Master of Wine examinations, are expected to use commonly accepted terms.

At the back of this book is a glossary of terms commonly used, whether for the dimensions or the flavors of a wine. At this early stage it is useful to distinguish between the words "aroma" and "bouquet." The relatively simple smell of a young wine is described as an aroma, but as it ages in the bottle and develops a more complex set of smells, this combination is known as its bouquet.

"SPICY" GEWÜRZTRAMINER GRAPES
IN ALSACE.

Three pointers to quality

Sweetness, acidity, tannin level, and body give you the dimensions of a wine. The flavor is the vital clue to its character. But if you want to be able to pick out wines you particularly like, and avoid the mean ones, it is helpful to know about three final aspects of wine that can be judged by the nose and mouth, and which point directly to quality or lack of it.

1 Cleanliness

The first of these is rather negative. A wine is described as clean if it has no obvious faults. Your nose is by far the best judge of this. If after the first sniff you feel you still want to go on, then the wine is clean. When I started writing about wine in 1975, about half of all wines smelled unclean and exhibited some fault or other. Now that the technological revolution has swept through most of the world's cellars, fewer than 1 percent of all bottles available in the international marketplace exhibit a winemaking fault. The most common fault, corkiness, has nothing to do with inept winemaking; it is simply the chance result of a tainted cork. Here are the most common nasty smells you might find in a wine.

TCA

This is shorthand for a particularly foul-smelling compound, trichloroanisole, given off by wines stoppered by a tainted cork. Such a wine will smell musty, moldy, and just plain horrible. The most common cause is a cork which has somehow during the harvesting and treatment process become tainted. Such a cork will not necessarily smell terrible itself, but it manages to imbue the wine with the nasty odor. TCA can strike any cork of any quality, although some wine producers believe that their cork suppliers take more trouble than most and minimize the incidence of cork taint. The incidence was so high in the late 1990s that many wine producers and retailers switched to plastic corks, which may eventually let air in and are non-biodegradable but never harbor TCA. The moldy smell associated with corkiness can grow in a wine once the bottle has been opened, and different tasters vary in their sensitivity to it. A corked or corky wine usually lacks fruit and charm on the palate.

TCA has also been found in wines made or stored near wood, beams, or pallets that had been treated with a particular chemical.

**ESTIMATES OF THE PROPORTION OF TAINTED
CORKS VARY BETWEEN 2 AND 5 PERCENT.
PRODUCERS HOPE FOR 0 PERCENT.**

This was a problem for some French wines (Château Ducru-Beaucaillou in St. Julien and Château Canon in St. Emilion, for example) in the late 1980s and early 1990s but it has since been successfully eradicated.

Sulfur dioxide

The smell that catches the tip of the nose or back of the throat like a recently struck match or a solid-fuel stove sometimes lingers over wines that were treated to a high level of sulfur at some point. Sulfur dioxide is the winemaker's antiseptic and is used to some degree in virtually all wines. Sweet and semi-sweet wines with considerable residual sugar may be treated with high levels of sulfur dioxide to stop them refermenting. The smell is therefore common in cheap sweet whites and in some German wines. It usually disappears with time (top German producers reckon you should keep their wines for years and years) or if you swirl the wine around in the glass, but asthmatics can react badly to sulfur and even I have found that now winemakers are using much less sulfur than they used to, I really notice the throat-parching effect of more traditionally-made German wines the morning after.

Rotten eggs/rubber

This smell, of the compound hydrogen sulphide or H_2S, is sometimes found in red wines which have been made in hot climates without enough access to oxygen. If left untreated it can develop into the positively sewage-scented compound mercaptan, but a mild level of hydrogen sulfide in a wine can dissipate if the glass is well aerated by heavy swirling—or by dropping a copper coin into the wine. Because this was a common fault in red wines made in the hotter parts of Australia, Australian noses seem particularly susceptible to mercaptan.

Brettanomyces

This is California's favorite fault, a mousy, horsey smell that can be even more pronounced on the palate and is the result of bacteria that may linger in old wood or less-than-spotless cellars. Some American producers even deliberately encourage a hint of "Brett," in the belief that it adds some "European" complexity to fine reds.

Oxidation

Recognizing this takes a bit of familiarization. Sherry and madeira are deliberately oxidized, i.e. exposed to oxygen, something which is usually avoided in winemaking. Oxidation is a fault in light wines and makes them taste and smell flat and stale. You can recognize oxidized wine because it goes brown, just like a cut apple exposed to oxygen. "Maderized" is almost synonymous, but used chiefly for white wines.

Acetic/vinegary/"pricked"

A wine that has gone even further than oxidation and already started to turn to vinegar as well as smelling like it.

Volatile acidity

The whisper "VA" goes up occasionally in the tasting room when a wine is obviously unstable or just about to become so. All wines with

Corked wine

It would be a waste of money to buy bottles to demonstrate wine faults. Instead, try befriending a local restaurateur, wine merchant, or the manager of the local wine store and ask for any bottles that are returned because of a fault. There is no shame in a corked bottle. It is not a sign of poor winemaking, merely of bad luck and/or carelessness on the part of the cork supplier.

You should never encounter cork taint from a plastic cork (though it may be much more difficult to restopper an open bottle with a plastic copy of a natural cork). Once you've smelled TCA once, you should never forget it.

Sulfur

To familiarize yourself with the two sulfur-inspired stinks, try to memorize the two very different smells of a hard-boiled egg left out for a day or two (H_2S) and that of a recently struck match or solid fuel cooker (SO_2). If you do come across a wine smelling of H_2S (maybe a cheap North African red?), try the copper coin trick.

Oxidized wine

Leave some not very precious wine standing out in a glass for a couple of days, somewhere you pass through regularly such as the kitchen. Every time you pass it, take a sniff and notice how it changes. The wine will gradually lose its fresh, fruity aroma and begin to go stale. Then the flavor goes flat and it becomes distinctly unappetizing. This is oxidized wine. The wine will eventually turn to vinegar, and along the way it can be described as acetic. You might like to remind yourself by smelling a bottle of wine vinegar.

The time this deterioration takes varies tremendously. Fortified wines like sherry and madeira deteriorate very slowly. In general terms, the more body a wine has the longer it will stay fresh. Some very concentrated, tough young wines—some youthful Australians, Californians, and especially Barolo and Barbaresco—can seem more attractive after a day or two of being exposed to air, but then start to decline like other wines. In general, Pinot Noir–based wines decline faster than those based on Cabernet Sauvignon. Grenache-based wines tend to decline fast too. (See pages 69–71 for more on air, wine, and decanters.)

Volatile acidity

Try to get a fix on the high, heady, almost nail polish smell that is common to some port (though not tawny), some of Australia's most alcoholic Shirazes, and some rustic reds made in particularly hot climates. These wines, while not being faulty, have a high level of volatile acidity.

a smell are volatile to a certain extent, otherwise they wouldn't produce a vapor for us to smell. But very old or very alcoholic reds can smell as though they are hurling so many messages at you there can't be anything left in the glass. Ports and Australian and Italian reds made in hot climates have particularly high levels of VA, or "volatility."

Carbon dioxide

If a wine looks and smells gassy and cloudy, it is probably refermenting—although many wines, especially young whites and rosés from hot climates, including many White Zinfandels, are deliberately bottled with a little bit of gas in them to make them taste more refreshing. In this case, they will be crystal clear.

Cardboard

This sign of filter pads' being changed too infrequently is, happily, rarely encountered nowadays.

Geraniums

This reminiscent whiff is a sign that a wine has been coarsely treated with sorbic acid.

Don't go around with wine faults up your nose. It would be a great shame to spoil your drinking pleasure by anticipating any of the off-smells detailed above. If a wine has one, it will impress itself on you soon enough.

2 Balance

A wine is well balanced if all its components blend into the whole with none standing out. A wine could be out of balance because it has too much acidity, because it is too sweet, because the tannin is too evident, or because the alcohol dominates the flavor. There is no single sensation that can help you make up your mind about whether or not the wine is balanced; you simply have to weigh up all the individual components. All good wines should be balanced by the time they are ready to drink, but a wine that seems to have a great future ahead of it may well be unbalanced in its youth simply because it is too tannic at that stage in its evolution.

Note whether the wines you drink in future are well balanced. "Harmonious" is another word used to describe wines whose components make up a pleasurable whole. Balance has nothing to do with price or status. Even very modest wines can be perfectly balanced, and many venerable greats are distinctly unbalanced in youth because the tannins are still too dominant.

3 Length

Another sure sign of wine quality is what tasters call the length or finish of a wine. If, having swallowed (or spat out) a wine, you're still aware of its flavor lingering in your mouth and nose—in a good way, of course—then the wine must have been well made. A mouthful of great wine can seem to hang about for minutes, if not hours, after the liquid has gone. This is why, in terms of total amount of pleasure given, expensive wines are not always poor value compared with lesser liquids whose impact is lost once they are swallowed. Each mouthful just lasts and lasts.

Take time to monitor how you feel just after swallowing a mouthful of wine. You could find that you can double the pleasure a wine gives you by positively enjoying its "long finish." Wines that "finish short" won't give you this added extra, and you might find yourself gulping them instead of savoring them.

THINKING WHILE DRINKING...

ALL WINE IS WORTH A LOOK.

The eyes don't have it

Standard texts on wine tasting point out at an early stage that three organs are involved: the eye, nose, and mouth, in that order. So usually they start with a detailed exposition of what the sense of sight can reveal about a wine.

Literally looking at a wine is indeed the first thing professional tasters do, and it can often give them vital clues if they're tasting "blind" (not knowing what the wines are). But this book is about tasting for enjoyment and, beautiful though the rich red of a well-made red Bordeaux and mellow yellow of a mature white Burgundy may be, the pleasure that our eyes can give is as nought compared with what the nose and mouth can do for the voracious amateur. For that reason, this section on "winesight" is relegated to third position after wine in the mouth and up the nose, even though you are more likely to apply your eyes to a wine first.

Sight reading

The only vital role played by the eye of someone who's tasting for pleasure is an obvious one: anticipating a fault. If a wine is hazy, it is usually suffering from some sort of malady and will not taste very good. If a wine, red or white, is much browner than you would expect it to be, then it is probably oxidized. If it's full bodied and slightly sparkling, then it could be going through unintentional second fermentation in the bottle. This will make it taste worse than it should (though the slight "prickle" in many lighter whites and reds is designed to refresh).

Wines that are meant to be slightly sparkling include:

Whites

Anything described on the label as "petillant," "perlant," or "frizzante"; Vinho Verde; some adventurous dry Italian whites designed for early consumption; many youthful little numbers from Australia, New Zealand, South Africa, and California—especially Rhine Riesling, Chenin Blanc, blush wines, and anything else with a bit of residual sugar in which the gas is deliberately retained to make the wine refreshing.

Reds

Slightly sparkling reds are much less common than white, but Lambrusco, red Vinho Verde (rarely exported) and the odd Chianti are allowed a little "prickle."

Harmless deposits

Most particles found in wine are quite harmless, merely a nuisance if not picked out (if they are lighter than the wine) or allowed to settle at the bottom of the bottle before it is poured (if they are heavier). Tiny bits of cork or deposit from the lip of the bottle that fall into your glass signify nothing more sinister than the fact that the bottle was opened and served rather carelessly. White crystals in white wine and fragments of dark deposit lurking in reds are also equally innocuous. Although they look so different, they are actually very similar, harmless solids that are precipitated by the maturation or storage of the wine, usually little crystals of tartaric acid. The tartrates are dyed dark red by the pigments in red wine, but in white wines they can look suspiciously like sugar or glass fragments to the wary wine-buying public.

Because the wine trade is heartily sick of having bottles returned in this innocent condition, many commercial producers now do their best to avoid it by freezing out the tartrates in advance, or else they remove them by heavy filtering. However, we wine fans always rather warm to a wine that has a deposit because it shows that the wine has not been overtreated.

If you want to convince yourself about the harmlessness of these crystals, try chewing them next time you encounter any in a white wine. You'll find that they taste very acid—which is, in fact, what they are, tartaric acid—and not at all sugarlike. Note the similarity of the taste to that of your trusty carton of cream of tartar. Red-dyed crystals taste much the same, but seem even crunchier.

**NOT DANGEROUS OR CARELESS, BUT
A PRODUCT OF NATURAL WINEMAKING.**

Visual clues

Now for the Sherlock Holmes part of the course. Those interested in becoming a whiz at blind tasting read on, for the sense of sight will be as useful to you with your wine glass as it was for the great detective with his magnifying glass.

At first glance

If the color of the wine is rather dull and homogeneous—if it doesn't seem to vary much between the center of the glass and the rim— then it's probably a particularly ordinary specimen. Most good wines actually look interesting, shining bright with nuances of color shading out toward a lighter rim. This is especially true in mature reds. The older a wine is, the greater the difference will be between the color at the center and an almost watery rim. If the wine has a very slight sparkle, then it could be any of the wines that are listed on page 43.

To get the best look at a wine's color, tilt the glass at an angle of 45 degrees away from you, against as light and plain a background as possible. A white tablecloth would be perfect, or even a white plate. In this respect, the average dinner table or sitting room is often not well geared up for optimal tasting conditions. You won't get much of an idea about delicate nuances of shading by candlelight, or against a wooden table, but then you probably won't want to try blind tasting in such circumstances. Bear in mind that if you're going to make a serious attempt at

guessing what a wine is, you (or the person who's trying to test your skill) should give serious thought to lighting. There is more about this on page 48 and page 58.

YOU CAN'T BEAT A PLAIN WHITE SURFACE.

THE DEEPER, PURPLER WINE ON THE LEFT IS MUCH MORE YOUTHFUL THAN THE MORE ORANGEY ONE ON THE RIGHT.

Second sighting

In terms of hue, "red" wines tend to go from purple to crimson to brick with age, while "whites" can start off colorless but usually become yellower and then browner as they age. The best clue to a wine's real hue is often to be found just inside the watery rim. This is particularly true in very deep-colored red wines which may be almost black except just here at the inner edge. With red wines, color is a prime indicator of their state of maturity. Anything with a bluish tinge must be fairly youthful; the merest hint of yellow or orange suggests age. The more subtle gradations in color there are at the rim, the older the wine. Color is rather less revealing about the identity or maturity of white wines. Most whites fall into that narrow band of color between pale straw and pale gold, and although they do tend to deepen with age, their color changes much less dramatically than that of reds.

Particular colors are associated with particular areas or grape varieties:

Reds

Purple most youthful wines of quality meant for aging.

Cherry many light reds made from grapes such as Pinot Noir, Gamay, Grenache, Merlot; also Beaujolais, Chinon, Bourgueil, Valpolicella, and some New Zealand reds.

Crimson: typical red wine color, so not many clues from this.

Mulberry if the color is deep, too, (see page 48) then the wine may well be made from the Nebbiolo or Syrah grape, or it could be a hot-climate Cabernet Sauvignon.

Reddish brown this wine will probably be mature. An orange tinge is characteristic of Nebbiolo-based wines such as Barolo, Barbaresco, and Brunello di Montalcino. A blackish tinge suggests the wine might be from South Africa or Australia and, though mature, may not be old.

Whites

Almost colorless Colombard, Chenin Blanc, Soave, Muscadet, very young Chablis or an inexpensive commercial blend.

Greenish tinge if the wine is also pale then probably German; if it is greenish gold, often Australian.

Pale, pale yellow standard color for most young dry whites.

Yellow gold in Europe, the extra color indicates sunshine or age, or some residual sugar. Even very youthful Chardonnays made in California and Australia tend to have this color, and the grapes Gewürztraminer, Pinot Gris, Sémillon, and Viognier usually produce deep-hued white wines wherever they are grown.

Deep gold great sweet wines can even go brown with age without deterioration.

Pinks

Can vary enormously in hue and depth. A purple tinge suggests ultra-modern winemaking, an orange one possible oxidation. But blind tasting pink wine is almost a contradiction in terms. If ever a wine was made not to be taken seriously, it is rosé.

theory

A third peer

Not only hue, but intensity of hue is an important clue. Red wines get paler with age (except for some wines from the amazing Domaine de la Romanée Conti, which take on a mysterious blush in their teens). A very deep color in a red suggests that it is either very young, made from thick-skinned grapes and therefore from close to the Equator or from an exceptionally sunny vintage further away, made so as to extract maximum color from the skins, or made from a grape variety such as the Nebbiolo, Syrah, or Cabernet Sauvignon in a ripe year. A red might be pale because it is old, or made far from the Equator or in a vintage which suffered from excessive rain just before harvest.

Conversely, depth of color in a white wine indicates age. It may also suggest that the wine is relatively sweet, or has been tinted by contact with oak, possibly oak chips (see page 99).

practice

The best way to get an accurate measure of the depth of color is to put a glass of wine on a white surface and look down into it from directly above. With samples of the same quantity, you will notice a surprisingly wide variation in intensity. Cabernet Sauvignon and Syrah/Shiraz-based wines will generally be much deeper than those made from Pinot Noir, Gamay, and Grenache. In general, the riper the grapes, the deeper the color will be. And the further away from the Equator the wine is from, the paler it will be.

theory

A fourth twirl

The final trick is simple, in fact rather a dashing thing to perform and sound off about at the dinner table. By swirling the wine around in your glass and watching the sides of the glass afterward, you will notice a wide variation in how viscous, or sticky, each wine is. Very viscous wines leave streams of something that looks like gin or clear nail polish falling slowly down the inside of the glass. Viscosity is a good indicator of body or weight, and therefore of a high alcohol content, lots of extract, or both. Light-bodied wines will not usually leave much trace on the sides of the glass, whereas full-bodied wines leave very much more pronounced streams, sometimes called tears or even legs (though this last term was surely thought up to ballast all that "wine is like a woo-man" analogizing). Low-temperature fermentation tends to increase viscosity slightly, however.

This swirling business is much easier to do with a glass that has a stem (one of the reasons why stemmed glasses are favoured for wine tasting). With your preferred hand, clasp the glass by the stem using your thumb and as many fingers as you like (see below).

Gently rotate the glass around a vertical axis so that wine splashes up the sides (see above). Now put the glass down and look at the insides of the glass. Are there great sticky streamers or just slight patches of dampness? (If the former, the alcohol level is high.)

The tasting technique
—a summary

Eye it up

First, look the wine squarely in the glass. If you are tasting for enjoyment, you can merely look to make sure the wine is clear and not fizzy if it is not meant to be. You can also take careful note of its color or hue by tilting it away from you at an angle of 45 degrees against a white background, and examine the depth or intensity of this hue by looking at the glass from directly above, as previously outlined. If you are trying to identify the wine, or get some measure of its quality, then these last two exercises are invaluable. Although authorities could talk for hours about the different hues and shadings they associate with different wines, in practice this "seeing" stage usually takes only a few seconds.

On the scent

Now to the all-important smelling, or "nosing." You could simply lift the glass to your nostrils and sniff, but a much stronger vapor is given off if you swirl the wine around a bit, as already described for testing viscosity on page 48, just before sniffing. The volatile elements that make up the vapor are given off at the surface of the wine, so by swirling you maximize the amount of wine in contact with air and encourage the volatile flavor compounds to leave the wine and collect just above the surface of the wine. You could simply jiggle the glass from side to side, but you would be in more danger of spilling some of this precious liquid than if you move it around rhythmically. It doesn't matter, by the way, whether you keep the glass in contact with the table while you swirl or do it in midair—though airborne swirling means you can get the glass to your nose even faster.

Some ultra-traditional tasters hold the glass by its foot rather than its stem, but I cannot see any scientific reason for this.

Nose first

Now get the nostrils hovering over the surface of the wine, preferably with the glass tilted at 45 degrees toward you to maximize the wine's surface area and therefore its impact. If the nose hovers just over the top of the glass, it will be able to benefit from all the vapor that collects inside it. Practice will probably show you that the best way to nose is to concentrate on nothing but the wine for a moment and then to take one short sniff. Shutting your eyes at this point helps enormously to get the most out of the wine, but it does make you look a bit silly.

When nosing, you should first do an almost subconscious check that the wine is clean. The message "I am obnoxious" will get to the brain fast enough if necessary, so you hardly need expend thought on this before going on to the whole point of smelling the wine: to experience its flavor. As we have seen, the olfactory center, our personal flavor-detecting agency, is located at the top of the nostrils. Luckily for blind tasters, and for those of us who like

I TRY NOT TO LOOK SILLY WHILE GETTING THE MOST OUT OF EVERY WINE.

A GOOD
MOUTHFUL
IS ESSENTIAL.

making comparisons between different wines, its signals appear to arrive in the brain close to that bit we call memory—which is why smells can be so uncannily evocative, and why wine tasting can be so much fun. Try to develop the ability to identify smells or flavors, to assess them qualitatively and to program them into your memory so that you can relate them to other smells in the future. Don't worry if at this point you feel confused about actually describing them. There are guidelines for individual wines throughout the second half of this course.

The first sip

Now at last you are allowed to get some of the wine into your mouth. It will make a composite impression on you of sweetness, acidity, tannin level, and body via the tongue and insides of the mouth, and will confirm the flavor by way of the vapor that gets up the retro-nasal passage. To make sure all the areas of your mouth most sensitive to each of these four taste dimensions are well exposed to the wine, you will need to take a fairly generous mouthful. For the same reason, hold the wine in your mouth for a little while before either swallowing it or spitting it out. (See page 79 for details of when this apparent sacrilege is recommended.) If, when you have some wine in your mouth, you open your lips slightly and take in some air at the same time, you will further encourage the wine's volatile elements to vaporize and pass up the retro-nasal passage to the olfactory center—thereby maximizing the impact any wine can make on you at any one time. This is why some enthusiastic inhabitants of the professional tasting room make such unsavory and unappetizing gargling noises. This practice should be avoided in the dining room.

Weighing it up

While the wine was in your mouth, you should have had a chance to weigh up each of the taste components and work out your assessment of its balance; and, as you consider how your mouth feels after you have swallowed or expectorated, you should notice its length of flavor.

All of that tasting technique took some time to explain, but it takes only a second to do. Just that simple technique will ensure that the relevant receivers are tuned in for every message a wine has to transmit. By nosing the wine first, you can experience all the pleasure of its flavor unencumbered by the distractions of the liquid in the mouth. By the time you have a mouthful of it, you are well equipped to understand the coarser but important messages transmitted there.

However, it is important to realize that tasting is extremely subjective—not only psychologically, in that we all like different wines and would choose different words to describe their flavors, but also physiologically, in that our sensitivities to different aspects vary enormously from person to person. Some people can find it very difficult to assess sweetness, for instance, whereas I am not particularly sensitive to sulfur (although my throat increasingly reacts to high-sulfur German wines the morning after). There are all sorts of weird explanations for this. Physiologists have worked out that the reason some people take lots of sugar in their tea and coffee is that the tips of their tongues don't actually come into contact with the liquid. By being "taught to drink properly" they can dramatically lower their sugar intake. My theory about my own sulfur insensitivity is that I was brought up in a house equipped with a coke-fired Aga. Don't laugh; it could well be right.

2. Practical matters

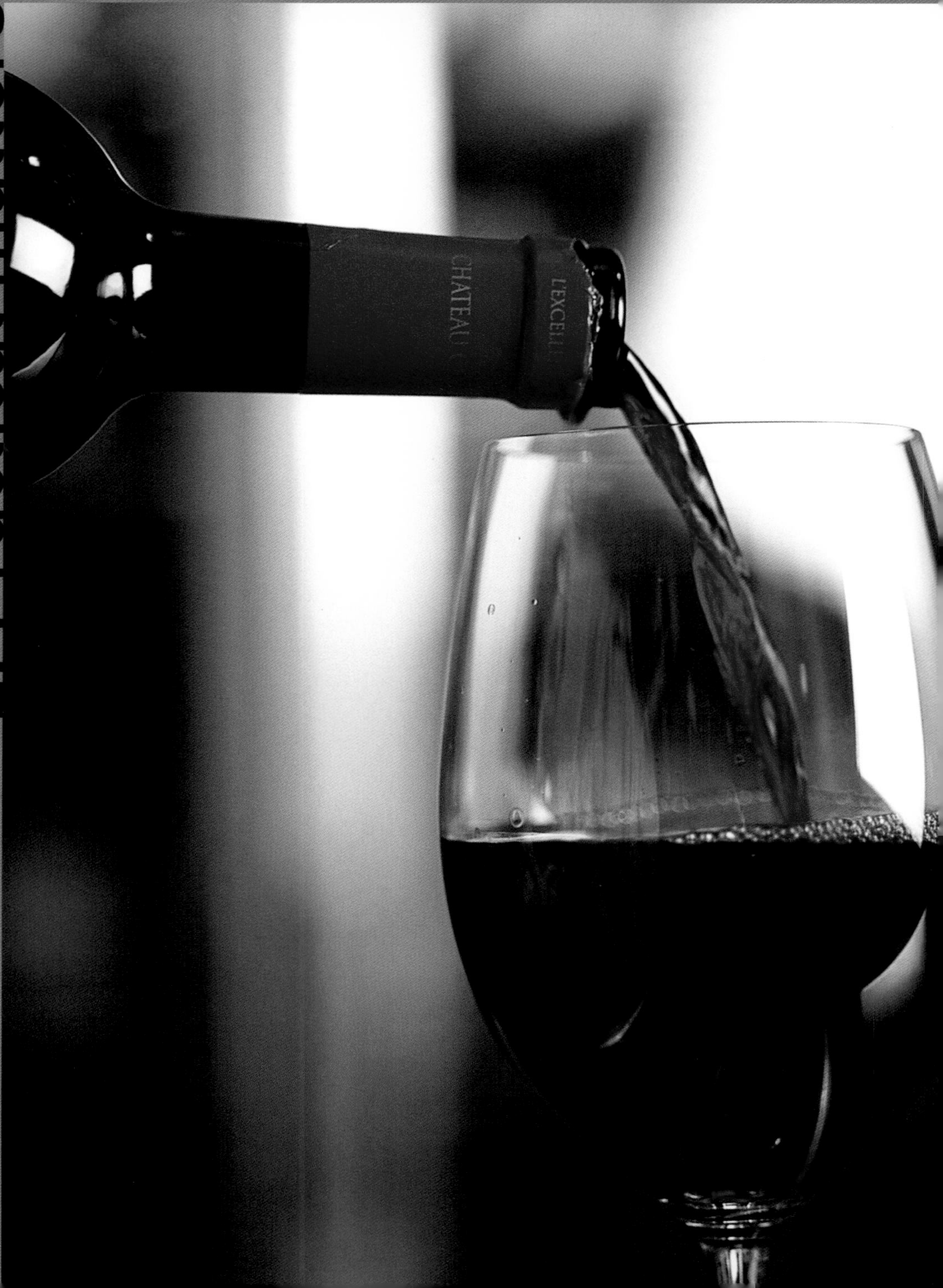

The tasting experience

You now know how to taste wine, a more rewarding yet hardly more taxing business than merely drinking it, and can use every tasting opportunity as part of this course.

The circumstances in which you taste may vary from the most clinical lab conditions (the sort of blindingly white atmosphere in which professional quality-control tasters work), through the various rooms of your house, to picnics. This chapter describes the ideal conditions for tasting, including the ideal equipment and practices as well as the ideal surroundings. Of course you won't always be able to taste under these perfect conditions. Indeed, you will make yourself extremely unpopular with your friends and family if you insist on complete silence at the dinner table as the wines are tasted, or on the perfect wine glass at a picnic. Adaptation and compromise are the keys to a satisfactory wine tasting experience0000. Your wine tasting experience will not be completely ruined if conditions are less than ideal, even though specialists can be dogmatic about this. If necessary, go ahead and make simple changes to your pre-wine-tasting lifestyle, but it would run counter to the philosophy of this book if your pursuit of the grape and its delights made anyone else feel uncomfortable.

Our senses are keenest early in the day, perhaps not from the moment we first raise an eyelid but certainly toward the middle of the morning. This is why professional wine tastings have traditionally been timed for late morning. However, there are few of us whose lives can easily encompass something as relaxing as a wine tasting in the first half of the day. In practice, you will probably do most of your wine drinking during, and just before, meals and will be at your most enthusiastic about wine in the evening. If you are thinking of trying some serious wine tasting, either by yourself or with friends but without the distraction of a meal, then try a Sunday morning tasting. During the rest of the week, when daytime tasting is difficult, early evening is better than late. Wine, as doctors well know, stimulates the appetite (there was a time when doctors specifically prescribed wine). Wine tasting therefore makes a good prelude to eating; if you leave it till after you've eaten a heavy meal you will find that your senses will have lost the keen edge so useful to the wine taster.

practice

Timing
Next time you have a day to
yourself—at the weekend perhaps
or, even better, when you're on
holiday—try tasting a single wine at
different times of the day. Write
down your impressions on each
occasion (there is more on tasting
notes on pages 76–78) without
looking at what you've written
previously and see if you can tell
when you were at your most
perceptive (actually perceptive as
opposed to apparently so). You'll
probably be in peak condition

toward the end of the morning, just
as you start feeling ready for lunch.
I certainly know from experience
that the first wine of the day
usually tastes the best, but that
rule did not hold good for the jug of
rich red I was once served with
breakfast on a Spanish wine
estate. You do need to be fully
awake before you appreciate that
first glass. Conversely, I am guiltily
aware of the amount of good wine
I have drunk at the end of the day
without fully appreciating every
nuance of its flavor.

theory

Physical environment

*If you want to get a good look at a wine's clarity, color, and intensity,
then you will need a surprisingly strong light and a plain white surface
against which to hold the glass. Strong daylight is best, but usually
impracticable. And even if you are able to taste during the day, sadly
you may be better off staying indoors. The great outdoors has a habit of
wafting the bouquet of a great wine into the far distance, and direct
sunlight overheats both wine and tasters.*

Each taster will feel differently about whether they taste better when
seated or standing. I don't find it makes much difference myself; my
nose and mouth seem blissfully unaware of what's happening to my
legs. But certainly, it's usually more comfortable to spit when
standing than sitting—if only to put the contents of the spittoon at
a greater distance from your nose and eyes.

Surprisingly few dining rooms make very good tasting
chambers. Candlelight is seen by advertising executives as
inextricably intertwined with wine drinking. This is possibly because
the candle is a conveniently portable light against which wines with
a strong sediment used to be decanted, and because wine is
traditionally associated with romance. But you need to have a lot of

WINE IS MADE FOR SHARING.

candles set pretty high above the table's surface to throw enough light for easy tasting. You can make the most of the light they give by using a white tablecloth, but you may well want to show off that beautifully polished table to your dinner guests. In these circumstances, a plain, light-colored plate should provide a suitable backdrop for wine examination. If all else fails, you can always hold a glass up to the nearest available light source for examination (this is the origin of that rather pretentious-looking stance in drawings of old-fashioned wine tasters). However, this doesn't give you nearly such an accurate and detailed impression.

Another good place for tasting at home is the kitchen. You may well have a useful white work surface that can easily be wiped clean of all wine's purple circles and blobs, and it may even be conveniently close to the kitchen sink (which would make a good spittoon if you can bear it).

Setting up a tasting

When setting up a tasting indoors, try to choose somewhere with plenty of soft light (not color-distorting strip lights) and work out how you are going to find that white surface. Ideally sit at, or even better, move round a table covered with a white tablecloth. Next time you buy placemats, plates, and table linen, spare just a thought for how useful a plain white surface would be when enjoying wine. Irish linen would be lovely, of course, but an old bedsheet or a strip taken from a roll of disposable paper table-covering won't make you taste any less acutely. Remember, too, that most tabletops need to be protected from the ravages of spilled wine by laying several layers of newspaper underneath the tablecloth. If you want to taste in a comfortable,

informal way in your favorite armchair—treating a couple of samples of wine as a substitute, say, for an evening paper—then there is an easy solution to the white surface problem. If you have your wine glasses on a side table next to you, you can simply hold them up against a piece of white card in your lap. An envelope will do, though if you are really getting into the swing of this, you'll probably want to write tasting notes and you can use the piece of card to write on.

Lighting

Look critically at the lighting over and near your table. Is there a way you could make it easier to get a good look at your wines without totally disrupting the room—perhaps by simply moving a standard lamp?

FEMALE WINE PROFESSIONALS ARE EXPECTED NOT TO BE FRAGRANT AT WORK.

Smells, scents, and fragrances

Because our noses are so important in wine tasting, it makes sense to distract them from the glass in your hand as little as possible.

Although convenient, the problem with wine tasting in the kitchen is the presence of strong smells. If you are trying to distinguish the difference between two glasses in front of you, it is made all the more difficult by a strong whiff of cooking or cleaning smells. This is why participants at formal tastings are expected to "come clean," untainted by scent or aftershave; why the organizers try to serve food only in another room; why there are so rarely any highly scented flowers, and why some hosts even place ostentatious no-smoking signs above the tasting table. You should hear the shocked whisper that goes up if a whiff of perfume or aftershave is detected.

Mine may be a rather heretical view, but I think the need for an olfactory vacuum in which to taste has been a little overstated over the years. We all have our own body smell; it can be so pronounced that others call it body odor, or it may be discernible only by very close friends indeed. We don't really notice our own body's smell—not knowing what life would be like without it, after all. We get used to our own little "aura." This is true even of heavy smokers who reek of stale tobacco. Those same people, I have noticed, are as able as the next person to distinguish nuances of flavor in wines, because they are used to tasting through their own tobacco-scented atmosphere. If, on the other hand, the heavy smoker says, "Here, taste this!" and hands you a wine glass he has been nursing for ten minutes, you will first smell him and only later, through the haze of his aura, the wine.

Similarly, a glass held by someone who purposely forswore the scent bottle before a tasting, but who always uses a fairly distinctively perfumed soap, will smell primarily of that soap and only then of the wine inside it to someone else. No matter what precautions are taken to make a tasting room as "unsmelly" as possible, there will be as many different little personal auras as there are people. Eventually the room will take on a smell, discernible to those with a keen nose, that is the mixture of all these together with the smell of all the wines that have been opened. There's no need, therefore, to get worried about the odd whiff of recently smoked cigarette or newly applied scent. It will soon dissipate and become just one component in the overall atmosphere—and our sense of smell is anyway constantly adjusting itself to its environment. If we hold the heavy smoker's or the clean-handed person's glass for long enough, we'll start compensating for their respective auras and start smelling the wine.

To ban the smell of food may be sensible when tasting clinically as part of a job or test, but food plays such an important part in the enjoyment of wine, it's unnecessary to bar it from every wine tasting. After all, at the dining table a wine's bouquet has to battle against the smell of the dish with which it is served, and this can be a much bigger problem than the odd plate of edible blotting paper that can be so appreciated by amateur wine tasters. Under such circumstances, you may find that dry savory biscuits make helpful tasting companions.

THERE'S NOTHING LIKE WINE FOR WORKING UP AN APPETITE.

Individual auras

Next time you're drinking wine with friends, swap glasses and notice how some people leave a hint of their own personal aura on a glass—sometimes a very strong hint indeed.

If you are a smoker, try not to smoke while someone else is concentrating hard on a wine, but don't despair in the fear that you'll never be able to taste as well as the nonsmoker. If you're a long-term smoker, try the blindfold test on page 12 at the same time as a nonsmoker friend. You will probably do every bit as well.

Room for distraction

Next time you're drinking wine, or otherwise using your nose, in an atmosphere where there is a particularly strong smell, notice how the smell that at first is so noticeable seems to fade with time. I've tasted wine in all sorts of circumstances—from southern European tasting rooms where the host almost invariably lights up a heady cigarette as you start to taste, to a room that was in the middle of being painted. At first I thought the wines would have no chance against the opposition for my nasal attention, but very soon I'd forgotten the distraction as my nose got used to the overall atmosphere. After all, people who live in towns where heavy pollution produces particularly noxious fumes don't even notice them.

When enjoying wine and food at the same time, especially hot or very aromatic food, the flavor of which drifts up into the atmosphere, try to work out your own practical way of getting the most from your glass of wine. You may want to turn slightly to one side, away from the food, when "nosing" the glass. Try to examine a wine before food gets to the table; it will show itself best without edible distractions.

So, a few ground rules when tasting wine

- To appreciate color, you'll need some sort of white surface.
- At a formal tasting you will be unpopular if you smoke or are obviously anointed with a strong scent or smell.
- In any surroundings you will find it easier to taste without the distraction of other smells, though in more social settings you may well decide you would rather sacrifice the fleeting aroma of Pinot Grigio for the exotic allure of your scent or the enveloping comfort of your favorite tobacco.

Possible distractions—
feeling right

*Before hoisting the no-smoking signs to limit other people's behavior,
make sure you are doing everything right for wine tasting. Far more
important than what is going on on the other side of the room is what is
going on inside your mouth.*

Before you begin, think about what you last ate and drank. Most
toothpastes make anything high in acidity tasted afterward seem
pretty awful. It would be a crime to taste a fine wine less than an
hour after brushing your teeth with minty toothpaste. Strong cough
and throat preparations can leave their mark in the mouth so
forcefully that wine tasting is difficult, as do strong mints and
chewing gum. Also, eating or drinking anything that is high in one
of the basic taste components most commonly encountered in
wine—sweetness, acidity, or tannin—seems to make assessing wine
soon afterward difficult. Chocolate, sharply dressed salads, and even
an apparently innocuous cup of tea seem to leave the mouth too
highly tuned into their own particular strength.

The simplest way to "neutralize" your mouth after one of these
problem tastes is to chew a mouthful of something absorbent but
fairly bland, such as bread, or to try to rinse out the flavor with water
(though I've found this less effective). I was once part of a tasting
group that met at eight o'clock in the morning (it seemed the
obvious solution for people who were working all day and studying
at night—at least I think that was the reason). The disadvantage of
toothpaste soon became apparent and so I took to brushing my teeth
without toothpaste and experimented with various mouthwashes,
with some success.

As well as having the inside of your mouth in order, it helps if
the inside of your head is also geared up for wine tasting. It's
amazing how one's ability to taste can be affected by mood. I know
how varied my concentration is at professional tastings depending
on the weather, my state of health, and what's going on in the rest of
my life. As outlined above, I think it helps to be very slightly peckish
to add that edge to your wine appreciation and you also need to be
alert and relaxed enough to concentrate, almost in your own little
world, on the wine in hand.

WINE TENDS TO MAKE FOOD TASTE EVEN BETTER.

But no matter what the main purpose of your tasting—identification, assessment, or straightforward enjoyment—you will find the most serious distraction from forming your own opinion will be other people. The whole business of wine tasting is so subjective, and even the most experienced tasters can feel so suggestible, that an early comment (delivered with sufficient confidence, of course) can sway a whole roomful of tasters. With any wine, your first impression—what you sense with the first concentrated sniff—is by far the most important. Allow yourself a moment of intense concentration as you nose a wine for the first time and take note of your reaction. If you think it's a Bordeaux and someone says, "Positively screams Burgundy, wouldn't you say?", don't allow yourself to be talked into smelling Burgundy on the second sniff. However knowledgeable other tasters may be, there is no reason why their judgments will be more accurate than yours. In my experience, it is the relative novices who often get things right in blind tasting. The old hands have far too many contradictory signals to confuse them. And newcomers are much more likely than us old hands to come up with a lively, telling description of a flavor, unfettered by jargon and convention.

Everyday tastes

Try, just once, the following immediately before taking a mouthful of wine:

toothpaste (it makes fruit juice taste dreadful, too)
cough medicine, drops, pastilles, or throat lozenges
extra-strong mints
chewing gum
chocolate bar
vinegar
tea

They each leave the mouth feeling different, usually hyped up to receive one particular message, and therefore not very good at making a sound critical assessment of a wine, let alone getting the full pleasure potential from it (although vinegar can, for instance, make an acid wine seem less acid, so hyped up are one's acid-sensing taste buds by the vinegar—see Chapter 6 for more on food and wine matching).

Preparing your mouth

Work out your own "neutralizing" technique so that you don't have to spend the rest of your life avoiding certain foods or preparations just in case someone might offer you a glass of wine.

Clearing your mind

If you reckon your palate and judgment are unswayable by tiresome details such as the weather or the telephone bill, then try a few simple exercises.

If it's the middle of winter, think of a wine you remember particularly enjoying in the summer—a beautifully refreshing light rosé or searing Sauvignon Blanc perhaps, something that brings back memories of sipping in the sunshine. Try tasting it on the next frosty day. Doesn't the wine now seem a bit thin, a little lacking in flesh?

If, on the other hand, you are currently enjoying a heatwave, try a rich red that gave you so much pleasure last winter. That high-octane Shiraz or Zinfandel that seemed so satisfying then surely seems a bit rough and overblown in warm weather.

Practise giving each wine that you drink just thirty seconds' attention as you approach it for the first time; that's thirty seconds during which your ears are metaphorically plugged, safe from the distraction of the environment and general conversation and, even worse, other people's comments on the wine.

The right temperature

The convention is that white wines and rosés are served cool, and red wines at a higher temperature somewhat loosely called "room temperature." It's useful to realize that this is very little more than a convention, and that by not sticking to it too rigidly you may be able to increase your enjoyment.

Generally speaking, the warmer a wine (or anything) the more volatile compounds it gives off and the more flavor it seems to have. There is an upper limit to this, however, as demonstrated by those restaurateurs who think that if a little warming is a good thing then lots of it will be very good. A red wine that's served too hot, say at 75°F (24°C), will start the irreversible process of turning acetic and breaking down. If you want to get maximum flavor from any wine— red, white, or pink—you should drink it at a temperature between 60° and 65°F (15° and 18°C).

There is another factor to consider: we cherish wine's ability to refresh us, as well as intrigue us with its flavor. Just as we like soft drinks to be chilled, we have come to expect aperitif wines drunk to refresh (which are usually white or rosé) to be chilled, too. And that custom has somehow been extended to encompass the chilling of all whites that we drink—even if it's a full-bodied white Burgundy to accompany a hot fish dish.

What determines whether or not a wine's flavor can survive chilling well is, in fact, dependent not on its color but on body. The more full bodied a wine is, the warmer it will need to be before its smellable components vaporize to yield its flavor. The lighter it is, the more easily volatiles are given off, even at lowish temperatures, and consequently it can be chilled to a lower temperature. Because white wines tend to be lighter than reds, the conventional wisdom of chilling them does usually work—but there are exceptions. Full-bodied whites, such as all but the thinnest Chardonnays, Viogniers, and Sémillons, great white Burgundy, white Rhône, and many massive whites from warm climates, will be spoiled by chilling them too assiduously. Conversely, light-bodied reds, such as simple Pinot Noir, Beaujolais, red Loire wines, many early maturing red Burgundies and north Italian reds, can be very attractive and refreshing to drink if slightly chilled.

Maximizing flavor

Take any red and any white wine, as basic as you like. Pour out two half-glasses of each and cover all four of them with plastic wrap to keep the bouquet in the glass. Put one red and one white into the fridge for half an hour and leave the other two in a normally heated living room. Now compare the two pairs, whites first and then red. When you take off the plastic wrap, you'll see how much more smell or flavor (and less acid and tannin) the warmer wines seem to have.

When to chill?

Next time you are drinking a chilled wine with food, try to work out what benefits you're getting from the coolness of the wine. Once the mixture of wine and food is in your mouth, it tends to warm up speedily towards body temperature—from 45° to 75°F (7° to 24°C) in ten seconds. Do you savor the wine for its refreshing coolness, or are you simply chilling it out of habit? Remember the exercise, described on page 12, of trying to distinguish between a red and a white wine when blindfold. If you found it difficult to tell them apart, why treat them differently when serving them?

Experiment by serving different wines at different temperatures to find out what suits you and the wines best. Of course, when you're drinking for refreshment you'll want the wine to be a bit cooler than when you're trying to eke the last ounce of flavor from it. Start gently edging up the temperature at which you serve full-bodied white wines. If they're good, you'll find them much more rewarding. If they're not so good, this will be demonstrated very obviously and you may decide not to choose that particular wine again. Try serving a light or low-tannin red slightly chilled, just like smart restaurants serve Beaujolais, and see how you can turn it into an inexpensive refreshing red aperitif.

Practical guidelines

The convention may also have something to do with the fact that heat tends to decrease our sensitivity to tannin and to acidity (and sulfur). That's why tannic red wines taste so tough if cool and why very sweet wines taste less so if very cool. Baron Philippe de Rothschild had the curious habit of serving his customary Château d'Yquem so cold with dessert that it had shards of ice in it. That insistence deprived him of its wonderful bouquet, just as overzealous wine waiters who try to keep their white wines permanently under 40°F (4°C) cheat their customers of much that the wine has to give.

If, on the other hand, you have a really nasty white wine, the best way to serve it is very chilled, as this will mask its nastiness. If you want to experience as much as possible of what a wine has to give, good and bad, then it is best to taste it at that convenient midway temperature known as "cellar," i.e. about 50° to 55° F (10° to 13°C). Reds can take rather higher temperatures than this, but the glass can always be warmed up quickly in the cup of your hand. Once served, the natural progression of the temperature of a wine is, after all, upward, by about 1° every three minutes until it reaches the ambient temperature. Once it's poured, it will be exposed to the hot air that inevitably surrounds all of us wine tasters, so don't worry if you fear you have served a wine at too cool a temperature, just realize how important it is to wait until it has warmed up enough to give its true flavor.

It is also worth pointing out that once wine gets into the mouth, it inevitably warms up in there. Experiments have shown that even heavily chilled wine rapidly thaws in the mouth, but by then it will be too late to get the full benefits of experiencing the bouquet in isolation.

A MIXTURE OF ICE AND WATER IS MUCH MORE EFFECTIVE FOR RAPID CHILLING THAN ICE CUBES ALONE, WHICH WILL TOUCH ONLY A SMALL PROPORTION OF THE BOTTLE'S SURFACE.

Storing and serving

You will want to evolve your own regimen on serving temperatures, but these are some general guidelines to follow:

Keep wine in an unheated room, or cellar, where the temperature doesn't vary too much during the day, or even from season to season. Ideal cellar temperature is about 50°F (10°C), though experiments involving keeping wines for long periods at much higher temperatures suggest it is the constancy of temperature that is more important.

For tasting purposes, most wines are fine served straight from a 50°F (10°C) cellar. Whites should reveal all, and reds can be swiftly warmed by being poured and cradled in the glass.

You may want to cool some wines, champagne and other sparkling wines for instance, well below 50°F (10°C) if you want to enjoy their refreshing aspect more than their flavor. You can put the bottle in the fridge for an hour or so, depending on how cool your fridge is. If this is an unplanned refresher you can chill the bottle by putting it into the ice box, or even the deep freeze, for about twenty minutes. This is supposed to give the wine too great a shock, but I have never known it to cause any more harm to the flavor than the standard method of immersing the bottle in an ice bucket or other roomy container filled with a mixture of water and ice cubes. Icy water works much better than ice cubes alone, by the way, because it means there's something cool in contact with every bit of the bottle's surface. If aesthetics are not a factor, ice-cooling sleeves kept permanently in the ice box, which fit around the bottle, work just as fast as ice buckets.

MAKE SURE THAT WINE IN LONG-TERM STORAGE IS PROTECTED FROM SUDDEN CHANGES OF TEMPERATURE.

The decanter
—vital or superfluous?

*There is still surprisingly little debate about serving temperatures for
wine; most drinkers continue to follow the accepted wisdom
unquestioningly. The Great Decanting Debate, however, still goes on
strongly and those following this wine course could well add useful
observations to it.*

The decanting tradition grew up from a time when wine was drawn
off into a jug from a cask in the cellar, and later when winemakers
left a deposit in the bottle. Then it made sense to pour wine off this
deposit into a decanter so that one could drink without chewing.
Nowadays, it still makes sense to decant those few wines that have
thrown a heavy deposit, provided they are robust enough to
withstand it. Some very old wines and some very lightly perfumed
wines would simply lose their bouquet if they had to suffer the fairly
boisterous treatment of being poured twice. This is akin to the
dangers already described of trying to serve a wine in the great
outdoors. Wine and too much air really do not make an especially
great mixture.

The debate centers on the question of how good a mixture
wine and some air is. For a long time it has been thought that the
process of aging in wine was simply one of slow oxidation, that small
amounts of air either already present in the sealed bottle or entering
through the cork gradually react with the wine to make it develop
into something more complex and ramified. It was thought
therefore that if you poured a bottle of wine into another container
such as a decanter, you would aerate it and somehow telescope the
aging process into just a few minutes by putting the wine into
contact with a lot of air. The bouquet would be fanned into life by
all this oxygen.

This view is still widely held, but the results of comparative
tastings of samples of the same wines opened and decanted at
varying intervals before tasting have been suspiciously inconclusive.
Furthermore, some authorities argue that the effects of aeration can
only be harmful; that by exposing a delicate bouquet to air you may
make it evanesce, and that the interesting reactions between oxygen
and wine are too complicated to be speeded up. All that can happen,

POUR CLEAR WINE OFF THE SEDIMENT WHICH
SHOULD BE LEFT IN THE BOTTLE. A CANDLE OR
STRONG LIGHT BEHIND HELPS.

they argue, is that the wine starts to oxidize too fast, and therefore it
begins to deteriorate.

Many ordinary wine drinkers claim that some wines, especially
cheap reds, taste much better if opened and not decanted but simply
left to "breathe" for a few hours. In fact, this may have nothing to do
with aeration. After all, such a small proportion of wine—only the
area of the narrow bottleneck—is in contact with air that only a tiny
fraction of the wine in the bottle could possibly react with oxygen.
A much more likely explanation for the improvement in taste is that
with very cheap wines there may be off-odors trapped in the gap
between the surface of the wine and cork (although this happens less
and less in our technically perfect age), and that this "breathing"
process allows them to evaporate.

It is true that the potential disadvantage of dissipating the
bouquet of a wine by decanting it or allowing a half-full bottle to
stand open for a while can sometimes be an advantage. Some wines,

full-bodied reds particularly, can be too intensely flavored when young. Rather than gaining extra flavors, the decanter allows them to lose some of their aggressive youth and mellow into a more palatable, if more vapid, middle age. This is especially true of some rich reds from California, Australia, Italy, the Lebanon, and the odd rustic wine from Spain and the Rhône.

Deciding to decant

A good set of rules is to decant a vigorous wine that is not more than twenty years old when there is a sediment to remove or a beautiful decanter to enjoy aesthetically, and otherwise not to get too exercised about the whole business. When I'm entertaining I tend to decant wines with a sediment just before guests arrive for entirely practical reasons—although if the wine is very old and delicate, say more than twenty years old, I would decant only just before serving. If once the wine has been poured, it is obvious that it is a bit "tight" and would benefit from aeration, simply swirl it around in the glass, which will be even more effective than the decanting process.

Is there a difference?

Very much an optional exercise, this, but one you can save for a rainy day when you feel like making a major contribution to what we know about wine and air. You'll need to open up a fair amount of wine, so it might make sense to try it out on a day when you will be entertaining in the evening. Choose any wine(s) you like, as many as you can afford, but even one will do. It would make sense to select a wine you normally would consider decanting—perhaps a very cheap red and a more expensive youthful one. You will need three bottles of each, I'm afraid. Open a bottle three hours before you plan to do your tasting and decant it into a decanter or a clean, empty wine bottle. Open the second bottle one hour before serving and simply let it "breathe." Open the third just before you begin the tasting. Now taste a glass from each bottle, served to you blind by your long-suffering, kind-hearted accomplice. See if you can notice any difference between the effect of the three different preserving treatments. This experiment is open to endless variation: with different wines, different lengths of time before tasting, and different sorts of "decanter" (something with a wide mouth, such as a glass jug, would expose the wine to more air than a narrow-necked vessel).

Leftover wines

As those marketing wine boxes or wine casks are very well aware, we don't always consume wine in exact bottle-sized portions.

If a wine is left in a half-empty bottle, the air will accelerate its deterioration. The lighter the wine the faster it will deteriorate. (Though, as outlined earlier, some very aggressively full-bodied wines can benefit from a bit of aeration.)

This book involves a great deal of comparative tasting, as it is chiefly by comparing a wide variety of different wines that we can learn about them. This is likely to result in wine leftovers, fractions of a bottle that you will want to keep for future drinking. Do not despair! Wine from a bottle that has been opened can last for weeks, provided it is kept in conditions as cool and as airtight as possible. The warmer it is, and the more air it is left in contact with, the sooner it will spoil.

The answer then is to keep a stock of small bottles, preferably of varied capacities, into which you can decant leftovers. Half-bottles are useful for this purpose, as are the quarter bottles served on planes and the half-liter bottles increasingly used for sweet wines. Fill them right up to the top and then stopper them firmly. Of course the decanting process itself will mean that the wine loses a little bit of its initial freshness, but it should still be enjoyable.

REACTIONS ARE SPEEDED UP AT HIGHER TEMPERATURES. CHILL LEFTOVER WINES IF YOU WANT TO KEEP THEM.

Choosing a glass

Even more important than the exact temperature of the wine, and certainly more important than whether you've decanted it, is the sort of vessel you taste it from.

Metal, and even pottery, goblets may look good on the shelf, but leave them there if you want to get the most from your wine. Glass is the ideal material for drinking wine because it is tasteless and does not impose any temperature on the liquid inside. You can easily warm up a glassful of wine by cupping your hand around it, if necessary, and you can savor the anticipatory pleasure of looking at a wine's color.

We have seen how important it is to swirl wine around in order to release its flavor, and this is where the stem comes in. A glass with a stem can easily be rotated, but without necessarily warming the wine up at the same time. You will want to "collect" the flavor in the space above the wine's surface, which means that the best shape for a wine glass is one that goes in from the bowl toward the rim. If you make sure the glass is not filled more than half full, there should be no danger of precious wine spilling out as you swirl and there'll be lots of room for the vapor to collect above it. The best wine glasses therefore are tulip- or near-spherical-shaped and have a stem. Colored glass is rather frowned upon as it disguises a wine's color; similarly cut crystal, the pride of glass departments throughout the world, for the same reason, and because it is heavy to swirl. For tasting, it's important that glasses are not too thimblelike, otherwise you won't be able to get the full impact "on the nose," as professional tasters say.

Remember that you don't need an enormous amount of wine in order to taste it, for it is the surface, rather than the depth, of the sample that releases the all-important flavor. An inch depth in an eight-ounce glass would be ample for tasting. The standard number of glasses for drinking (as opposed to tasting) per 75cl bottle is between six and eight, but you could easily squeeze out up to twenty samples for tasting purposes.

You don't need a battery of different glasses for different wines. You could get by quite happily with a single sort, described above, though you should probably fill it only sparingly when serving fortified wines as strong as port and sherry. Wine professionals' single-mindedness over glasses does waver a little when it comes to sparkling wines and champagne. Approved glasses for bubbles are tall and thin, allowing only limited escape space for the carbon dioxide (not those saucers which encourage wines to lose their fizz fast), but the standard glass will be fine for tasting sparkling wines—possibly better for enjoying the flavor as opposed to the fizziness.

Thin, delicate glass is not necessary for tasting, but it does add to the overall pleasure of drinking. The most hedonistic wine glasses are those made of the thinnest, most luxurious glass which seems to put you in most intimate contact with the wine. And if the glass is really fine quality, it can surprisingly be less fragile than a thicker, cheaper glass.

Anything but glass

Try drinking wine out of the following drinking vessels and note how "wrong" it tastes. Is it partly because you can't get a look at the wine before tasting it?

china teacup, pottery mug, pewter tankard, silver goblet, plastic beaker, paper cup (this, curiously, is probably the best of these, affecting the wine's flavor least)

Try swirling a sample of wine around in a glass without a stem. It will be much more awkward and liable to spill.

The right shape

Muster as wide a selection of differently shaped glasses as you can, and pour a small, similarly sized sample of any single wine into each. Give each glass a short swirl, taking a concentrated sniff from it immediately afterward: swirl, sniff, swirl, sniff, etc. Notice how much lighter and more evasive the bouquet is on those samples in glasses whose shape encourages the volatiles to escape into the atmosphere. The bouquet is much stronger, however, when it is trapped in more enclosed glasses. There is an official tasting glass devised by the Institut National des Appellations d'Origine (INAO), but the quality seems to be variable. Specialists in producing plain, well-shaped glasses made from attractively thin glass with wine drinkers specifically in mind include Riedel of Austria (which makes a myriad of special shapes for special wine types), Schott, and Spiegelau.

Do be careful when washing and storing glasses. You may well need to use detergent to get greasy finger-marks off, but be sure to rinse the glasses well afterward in clean water. The taste of dish detergent does nothing for fine wine—and its traces will play havoc with the mousse of a sparkling wine. I put my finest glasses in the dishwasher, but have found considerable variation between which washing products leave the least traces (powder seems better than liquid for some reason). Just to prove this point, next time you have some sparkling wine open, compare the intensity and speed of the bubbles in a thoroughly rinsed glass and one that still has a slight coating of detergent. You will find the fizz will be a damp echo in the second glass. Also be careful not to invert the glasses for storage, so that they don't trap a stale smell in the bowl, and in a clean cupboard or box.

theory

Wine and words

In order to compare, discuss, and remember wines we need some way of recording and communicating our reactions to them.

A vocabulary consisting of the delighted yelp and disgusted moan is enough if you want to keep your thoughts about wine entirely to yourself, but is not otherwise particularly helpful. An increasing number of tasters use scores or ratings, typically points out of twenty or one hundred, or perhaps alphas and betas or a certain number of stars.

Some wine tasters try to draw the impact of a wine's flavor on the palate.

Here is a wine that is very showy at first but then finishes short.

And here's one that is "dumb" on the nose but opens up in the mouth.

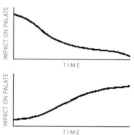

Either or both of these "languages" are fine to supplement but not supplant the most subtle method of communication that we can so far muster for flavor, style, and so on: the written (and spoken) word. At the back of this book is a glossary of common tasting terms, though you will doubtless evolve your own terms for some sensations. The most useful of these will be your "trigger" words for various commonly encountered grape varieties. Once these are established, you should be well on your way to successful blind tasting. In my early wine tasting days, I found that for some time I had used "blackcurrants" for the Bordeaux grape Cabernet Sauvignon and "raspberries" for red Burgundy's Pinot Noir, but was still searching around for a word I could use to pin together all my impressions of the Hermitage grape Syrah. Then someone volunteered their "burnt rubber," and it has worked ever since (though only for Syrah in relatively cool climates—not Barossa Shiraz from Australia, for example). This story is told to encourage you to persevere if you find matching words and flavors difficult. As you will have gathered, the expression can be as absurd as you like.

Keeping a record

Get into the habit of writing down your impressions of the wines you taste as soon as possible after you try them, at the time of tasting ideally, or perhaps when you get back home.

Using trigger words

Try to develop your own special trigger words for different grape varieties and then for the other more complicated aspects of wines. Throughout the second half of this course, specific examples are suggested to help you. But if you are stuck for a trigger word, try reading through your old tasting notes to see if any expression keeps cropping up in association with a particular factor determining taste.

Tasting notes

The easiest way to learn about how wine tastes is to keep a record of your tasting experiences, to make tasting notes on as many of the wines you taste as you can. Knowing that you have to describe a wine helps enormously to concentrate your mind on it, and the notes will provide a reference for you when building up the valuable experience of drawing comparisons. Quite how assiduously you keep up the note-taking habit will depend on how much enthusiasm you have. I don't make notes when friends ask me over for supper, but I know one or two professionals who do. They have never regretted it for a minute (their friends and spouses may have occasionally, but not their publishers). The difficulty of choosing words to describe wines has been outlined in Chapter 1, under "Capturing the flavor" on pages 33–35.

If you do most of your tasting in a fairly structured way, usually at home and occasionally out with like-minded friends, you could keep all your tasting notes in one book. If you persevere and taste a sufficiently wide range, you might find such a written record of your drinking experience to be extremely valuable one day. Loose-leaf binders are useful for those who taste more peripatetically, and there are now several programs available for those with the time and inclination to enter all their tasting notes onto a computer, which then allow easy retrieval and cross-referencing of information. "Now let's see…when did I last taste a Mondavi Cabernet?"

Keeping clear and consistent records

The most important item on your tasting notes is the full pedigree of the wine you are tasting. Make sure you eventually get down its name, vintage, producer, and any other information, even if you start out by tasting the wine blind. A set of random wine descriptions is of little use to anyone unless each wine is fully identified. If you are organizing a wine tasting for friends, you will help them enormously if you write out tasting sheets beforehand.

Make sure you leave plenty of room between each wine's name as full-blown tasting notes encompass descriptions of each aspect of the wine's full assault on the senses, usually categorized under the headings "eye," "nose," "mouth," and "conclusion." When starting out, it helps to be wordy rather than terse, so that you establish what sort of characteristics you normally associate with various groups of wines. As you get more experienced, you can begin to omit the features you've come to expect and note only the most striking aspects of the wine.

Wines change with age, so do try to date your tasting notes. And when reaching conclusions about a wine, take into account some assessment of how ready for drinking you think it is (the amount of tannin in red wines, and acid in whites, is a good pointer here) as well as how good it is. There is more on assessing wines on pages 86–87.

MY TASTING NOTES ARE FAMOUSLY ILLEGIBLE BUT COMPRISE A RECORD OF MY WORKING LIFE.

The noble art of spitting

It's heartbreaking but true: there are no tasting faculties in your throat, so you don't need to swallow wine to taste it.

In fact, the less you swallow, the less clouded your perceptions will be by the haze of alcohol and the better you will be able to taste. You may think that only after you swallow a wine do you get a proper perception of its aftertaste. But that's not taste, it's an afterglow—the simple and none-too-subtle effect of ethyl alcohol. If you spit out every mouthful, you will be amazed at how much more legible your tasting notes are at the end of a tasting.

I am not suggesting that you expectorate on social occasions. In fact, spitting out good wine seems as much a waste to me as it doubtless does to you. There are, however, some circumstances in which it is wise to spit out the alcohol, if possible—when you want to keep sober, either because you are driving or because of other commitments after the tasting; when you are tasting a dauntingly high number of wines, more than half a dozen, say, or when you are tasting very young wines that don't give a great deal of pleasure.

Losing inhibitions about spitting in public is one of the first things to be done by the embryonic wine taster. It is sad but irrefutable that wine, that wonderfully intriguing and uplifting liquid, contains a potentially toxic and dangerous substance. When it makes sense to spit, you should be proud rather than ashamed to do it. You may associate expectoration with rather seedy old men and pavements, but wine people have perfected the art of doing it with great style. "Spit with pride" might well be the wine taster's motto. The stylish spit is forceful, an elegant trajectory with not the merest suggestion of a dribble, aimed dead center of the spittoon.

Any old jug, or an empty bottle with a wide funnel in the neck, can earn itself the smart appellation of spittoon, though to avoid nasty splashes it makes sense to put some absorber like torn paper or sawdust into the bottom of it. A wooden wine case, such as those used by the better Bordeaux châteaux, filled with sawdust is a good spittoon, though a spittoon with running water is even more efficient at disposing of the unsavory evidence. If you can taste near a suitable sink then the business of spitting is easy. On anything but the most prosaic floor coverings, it is wise to spread plastic sheeting underneath and around any spittoon.

Taste and then dispose

Take a mouthful of wine, taste it as instructed so far—monitoring its effects on your mouth and brain—and then spit it out. Compare the sensation with that of monitoring the mouthful and then swallowing it. Is there really any difference in taste? Okay, swallowing the wine might leave a few more volatiles at the back of your mouth, well placed to waft up the retro-nasal passage, but the difference is marginal. Notice how fully you can experience the finish of a wine even if you spit it out.

Spitting with confidence

Practise spitting neatly in the bath. Put lots of force behind each spit, purse your lips and aim for your feet. You are not expected to spit in silence.

A word of warning. Even if you carefully spit out every single mouthful, you will probably not entirely escape the effects of alcohol. Come what may, alcoholic fumes will travel around your mouth, up your nose and retro-nasal passage, and you may feel slightly light-headed. In any case, you will find it extremely difficult not to swallow a single drop of wine (I have found that I tend to ingest about a glassful for every thirty wines I taste however hard I try to spit everything out) and all those fumes will further prejudice the results of a breathalyzer.

ME, SPITTING WITH PRIDE AND UNUSUAL NEATNESS.

Formal tastings

Here is a brief description of a clinically formal tasting so that you'll know what to do if invited to one, or if you want to organize a particularly classy wine tasting for friends.

As many as one hundred wines may be "on show" at such a tasting, though most tasters would not tackle them all. An open bottle of each is set out on long tables covered with white tablecloths. If the organizer has been thoughtful, the tables will be sufficiently well spaced to allow good traffic flow. Spittoons should, similarly, be strategically placed. Many's the time I've spent most of a tasting with cheeks bulging as I jostle my way through the crowd to the lone spittoon in the far corner. The odd jug or bottle of water to rinse glasses or palates is a good idea, as well as some edible but not too distracting blotting paper in the form of low-flavor savory biscuits. Chunks of neutral bread such as a baguette provide more useful ballast (wine tasting stimulates the appetite quite frighteningly). Little cubes of hard cheese are likely to flatter the wines but may sometimes distract.

White before red, young before old?

In most circumstances, even at the dinner table, there is a conventional order in which wines are served or tasted, and it generally makes quite a bit of sense. "White before red, dry before sweet and young before old" encapsulates it. As with serving-temperature considerations, "white before red" is really a loose way of saying "light bodied before full bodied," so that a wine is never overwhelmed by one that preceded it. It makes sense not to put dry wines at a disadvantage by coating your mouth with sweetness first (though the French almost always serve something sweet as an aperitif and somehow seem to survive). The older a wine, in general, the more fascinating it is (true only of fine wine, though—don't try "maturing" a cheap plonk). It is therefore sensible to ascend to a peak of quality as a tasting climax.

There are two good reasons for ignoring the "young before old" bit, however. One is if you plan to serve so much wine in such raucous circumstances that you want to showcase your finest wine while everyone is sober enough to fully appreciate it. The other is the result of the modern phenomenon whereby wine is being made increasingly alcoholic and concentrated. And in some of the newer wine regions quality is increasing virtually systematically with every vintage. In both these cases, the sheer weight or quality of the younger wines can overwhelm the older ones and so it can make sense to taste a variety from old to young. (This is the rule generally followed by professional tasters of the most concentrated wine of all, vintage port.)

Choosing the wines

At a tasting organized by a wine producer or retailer, the choice of wines will be dictated by those they want to sell to you. If you are organizing a tasting, you might well follow some of the suggested exercises in this course. Any tasting organized around a grape variety is always fascinating. It is relatively easy to find examples of, say, the Cabernet Sauvignon grape from all over the world, and by tasting each one you can learn a lot not only about the varietal, but also about the regions where they were made. You could also taste the range of wines made by a single producer to try to come to grips with each of them and his or her particular style. Some of the most fascinating and intellectual tasting exercises, however, are based on either a "horizontal" or "vertical" tasting. Tasting horizontally has nothing to do with reclining on couches, but involves studying lots of similar but different wines of the same vintage—all of the 1998 Pauillacs, for example, to see how Château Latour 1998 compares with Châteaux Lafite and Mouton Rothschild or, at a considerably lower cost, a range of the most recent vintage's Chardonnays from your favorite region. Tasting vertically involves tasting different vintages of the same wine; vintages of Château X 1995 back to 1985, for example.

How to serve

At a formal tasting you will usually be given your own tasting glass and be expected to make do with a fairly small tasting sample, up to 1 inch (2.5 centimeters) deep, of each wine, emptying any remains into a large "dregs" jug or bottle with a funnel before you make a start on the next wine. Sometimes, if wines or glasses are in very short supply, you may find there will only be a single glass of each wine placed in front of its bottle for everyone to taste from. A disease would have to be very rabid to manage to transmit itself from one taster to another via a glass rinsed in wine—alcohol being a strong disinfectant. If you are tasting as cozily as this, though, it really does make a bit of a stink if you leave the smell of cigarette smoke or perfume on the glass.

Quantities

You will probably find that the number of different wines you can study seriously in one session will increase steadily and then reach a maximum—quite literally, saturation point. I would suggest that you start by comparing only two wines at a time. The first exercise in specific wine tasting, contrasting two Chardonnays from different places (see pages 98–99), is a good starting point. Quite soon you will find you are able to look in detail at three wines, still getting enjoyment out of them without feeling overwhelmed.

The bigger the group in which you taste, the more wines you can collectively afford to tackle. You may find, though, that twelve at a time is the absolute maximum. Many professionals try to taste more at a time—sometimes as many as one hundred or even more. I think my own limit is about eighty a day, although this varies according to mood and circumstance, and it helps if they are wines of varied styles.

Food and wine

Try chewing a dry biscuit or plain bread between mouthfuls of wine and notice how little the food seems to affect the palate.

When planning which wines to serve with a meal (if it's the sort of occasion that warrants more than one wine), bear in mind the conventional sequence of wines. For more on this (actually very uncomplicated) subject, see Chapter 6, "Wine, food, and fun."

Directional tasting

You don't have to be a millionaire to indulge in one of these "directional" tastings. Bordeaux's rather formal structure of ranked châteaux lends itself particularly well to the technique, but the wines don't have to be *premiers crus*. Any collection of wines from a single vintage, no matter how humble the provenance, can give you a horizontal tasting, and will teach you something about that vintage. You can attempt a vertical tasting of any wine with a vintage date on the label—though it might take quite a bit of scouting about to gather together much of a collection of different vintages. Most wine retailers sell one or at best two recent vintages of a given wine and only a handful can offer a good range of mature vintages.

practice

OPAQUE INTERNATIONAL WINE CHALLENGE BAGS
MASK THE IDENTITY OF THE WINES BEING JUDGED.

Tasting "blind"

*Organizing a "blind" tasting is quite a lot of work, though the amount
you learn can make it very rewarding.*

It is absolutely staggering how important a part the label plays in the
business of tasting. If we know that a favorite region, producer, or
vintage is coming up, we automatically start relishing it—giving it
every benefit of the tasting doubt. In my early days it took me five
years of puzzlingly disappointing blind champagne tastings before I
realized that I didn't actually like the taste of young Bollinger as
much as its ethos and label. (I have subsequently learnt that even
non-vintage Bollinger is a wine that demands bottle age.)

With this in mind, you will need to ensure that no clues to
identity are given when enjoying a blind tasting. This may mean
painstakingly decanting every wine into a set of anonymous bottles,
though this would not be suitable for very delicate wines. (A fiendish

organizer of blind tastings of my acquaintance deliberately enjoys decanting grand mystery red wines into empty Château d'Yquem bottles that one normally associates with sweet white wine.) Otherwise, you will have to employ one of the bottle-disguise methods outlined below.

If you really get the wine bug, you may want to let the bug eat into your social life by serving wines blind when entertaining. (It's easier then because you can use decanters or a well-placed hand when pouring.) This can be great fun if everyone is interested in, and equipped for, guessing. It can also be extremely tedious, especially if the provider of the mystery bottle(s) refuses to give any clues or encouragement. Be wary of torturing your guests.

Masking the bottle

The simplest way to mask bottles (if they are shaped identically) is to wrap them in aluminium foil or to adopt the American technique of brown-bagging them. For this, you need a collection of fairly tough opaque paper bags or foil roasting bags into which you can pack each bottle, either taping the bags closed around the neck, securing with a rubber band or simply scrunching the paper up tightly. Remember to take all the capsules off completely so that there aren't any distracting identification signals. You'll need to give each bottle a number or a letter, either scribbled on the bag or swinging round the neck on a reuseable cardboard label. Oh, and if you are wrapping the bottles in foil, it is of course much easier to open the bottles after wrapping, so the masking sequence should be:

decapsule, wrap, open, shuffle, number, taste, panic.

Wine games

Australia's most vocal wine man, Len Evans, has devised a more socially acceptable variation on the guessing theme. In his Options Game, the host starts by asking: "Is it Bordeaux or Burgundy?" Everyone who gets that right can go on to a more detailed question such as "Is it Médoc/Graves or St. Emilion/Pomerol?" The Australians are so sharp they actually start at the next level of question, "Pauillac or Margaux?" The host might then go on to, "Is it pre-1990 or post-1989?", "1996, 1995, or 1994?" And finally, "Château Palmer, Issan, or Lascombes?" All pretty tricky stuff, but it is a game that even people who know nothing about wine stand a surprisingly good chance of winning!

Assessing quality

Blind tasting may be a fairly rarefied and not terribly useful skill, but some guidance on assessing a wine's quality can help you enjoy just a bit more every wine that comes your way.

This is particularly beneficial because price is no direct indicator of quality. There is no great wine available at bargain basement prices (although there are many good ones). There are, on the other hand, some very disappointing wines that cost a great deal, and there is an enormous variation in the quality of wines priced in-between these two extremes. It therefore makes sense to learn how to judge quality in an educated and rational way.

The two most obvious pointers to quality—balance and length—have already been outlined on pages 40–41. You can enjoy a fairly basic wine, a standard Chardonnay or Merlot for example, if it is well made. Look for the sensation in your mouth after you have swallowed or spat out a mouthful of the wine, as well as monitoring its flavor and how complex it is. A fine example of a Meursault or a Pomerol is likely to be an obviously "greater" wine, with more layers of flavor and intrigue, but there is a time and place for every sort of wine. There have been several periods of my life when I have been lucky enough to taste nothing but great wines for days on end.

EMPTIES—THE FINAL RESULT OF ANY WINE TASTING.

I wouldn't say it was pure hell, but by the end this ungrateful wretch was aching for a simple glass of something straightforward and everyday. We need variety in wine drinking as much as in anything else. Don't think that it is not worth learning about wine if you can't afford to spend very much. It is one of the ironies of the wine market today that just as the price differential between cheapest and most expensive bottles is greater than ever before, the difference in quality between these two extremes is probably narrower than it has ever been. There is good and bad quality at every price level.

Scoring the wine

To concentrate your mind on assessing the quality of a wine it helps to give it your own score as well as making the usual tasting notes. This is particularly helpful if you are tasting a range of similar wines with a view to picking out your favorites. After all, one of the chief consequences of informal comparative tasting should be to note the names of those wines, producers, and vintages that give you particular pleasure.

Most American tasters use points out of one hundred, although in practice a score below eighty is quite rare so it converts into a twenty-point scale—except that those who use a twenty-point scale tend to give anything that is not technically faulty at least twelve or thirteen points. Halves are often used within the twenty-point scale.

The most common problem with scoring is deciding whether to score an immature wine for potential or actual quality. My own tasting notes are littered with arrows denoting states of maturity. You may have to invent your own symbols. There is also much (thoroughly enjoyable) debate about how to score a pleasurable wine that is not necessarily typical.

Funnily enough, likes and dislikes, the one area everyone who doesn't know much about wine does invariably proclaim they know about, tend to recede slightly with the gaining of knowledge and experience of wine (sounds much grander than just drinking it, doesn't it?). Most professional tasters end up with more or less the same concept of what makes a good wine—although wine tasting is above all a subjective sport.

Happy tasting.

3. The raw material: white grapes

First know your grape

Curiously, only one sort of wine actually tastes like grapes, and that is wine made from Muscat or related grape varieties. In every other case, wine tastes quite different from grapes, even from those grapes from which it was made.

Grape juice has a simple fruity flavor, its lack of complexity sometimes being labeled "rather one-dimensional." Wine, on the other hand, has a much more complicated taste, definitely two-, possibly even three-dimensional. There are layers of flavor here, different nuances, though underneath everything there should be the same basic fruitiness that grapes have.

The winemaker's job is to transform the raw material, grapes, into something as interesting as wine, while retaining their common attribute, fruitiness. Grape skins taste astringent. The pips when crushed taste bitter. Only the flesh, which is mainly juice, is suitable raw material for a fresh, fruity white wine. (Red wines may need a bit of astringency or tannin—see page 27.) The first stage in making a white wine therefore is to eliminate the skin and pips from the process by gently crushing the grapes and running off the juice. The harder the grapes are pressed, the more astringency the resultant wine will pick up from the skins. Fine white wines are usually made from "the free-run juice," i.e. the juice that is drained from a vat of grapes crushed by their own weight (although some producers of otherwise rather neutral white wine deliberately give them a little "skin contact" to leech a bit of flavor into the wine).

Wine and grapes

"Nose" (i.e. smell) any of the following wines and notice how like the taste of Muscat grapes they smell. "Grapey" might be your first tasting note: Muscat, Moscato, Muscatel, Moscatel, Asti, Muscat d'Alsace. Arm yourself with a few grapes and a glass of wine to sip. Contrast the two flavors.

Tasting the grape

Peel yourself a grape. Taste the flesh. Then chew the peel, and nibble a pip. Notice how unpleasant the last two are without the flesh. These last two exercises are an uncommonly unpalatable part of this wine course.

theory

Grape juice contains sugar because the grapes were ripe and this can now be fermented into alcohol, turning sweet grape juice into a much drier liquid that can be called wine. (This is why grape juice is always sweet. The only way to get it "drier" is to ferment out the sugar.)

Yeast is the stuff that converts the sugar to alcohol. Yeasts occur naturally in the atmosphere of a wine region and may collect on parts of the grape. They are therefore naturally mixed into the juice in an established vineyard; or cultured yeasts may be introduced for even greater control over the process. When they have done their work they die, so wines very rarely taste "yeasty." This fermented grape juice is now wine although, as demonstrated below, it is capable of extraordinary variation of taste.

Gewürztraminer— the most recognizable grape

Gewürztraminer may be one of the most difficult grape varieties to pronounce (Guh-vurts-trah-mee-ner) and spell, and is far from the most common white varietal wine. But we begin our tour of the grapes with it because it is by far the most distinctive and easiest to imprint on your palate memory for future recognition.

It has a heady, almost perfumed, lychee scent. Some find it reminiscent of an unidentifiable tropical fruit. There's something definitely exotic about Gewürz (which is German for "spiced"), though it can pall after a while. Connoisseurs claim to find it too obvious—like a cheap perfume—after prolonged exposure to it, but it's a wonderful, safe starting point for the wine taster.

The "traminer" bit of its name is derived from the village of Tramin in the Italian Tyrol, and there are still some light, delicate Gewürztraminers made in the Alto Adige hills of northeast Italy. The most common Gewürztraminer, however, is from Alsace in eastern France, just over the border from Germany. Alsace is famous for its perfumed wines, which smell sweetish but actually taste dry (providing the exception to the rule that the palate usually merely confirms what the nose has already suspected). Alsace Gewürztraminers are a force to be reckoned with as they ripen well,

**PINK-SKINNED GEWÜRZTRAMINER GRAPES
MAKE DEEP GOLDEN WINE.**

but in most cases, the sugar in the grapes is fermented out to make dry, or at least dryish, wine high in alcohol, often as much as 13 percent. They smell lusciously pungent but have a dry finish. The grapes themselves are unusual in that many of them are pinkish-skinned, not white at all, and as a result Gewürz can often be quite a deep-coloured straw yellow. Low acidity is characteristic of Gewürztraminer made in a fairly warm climate, and some of them go rather "oily" with age.

In Alsace, Gewürztraminer is considered a noble but rather tiring grape, and the winemakers themselves often prefer to drink Riesling. It is also grown across the Rhine in the warmish German wine regions of Pfalz, Rheinhessen, and Baden (where it is often left quite sweet), and in Austria, where it can make delicious, deep golden, very sweet dessert wines. Most New World wine regions have experimented with this grape variety (and generally dispensed with the umlaut on the u). Some of the most successful examples have come from New Zealand and the Pacific Northwest of the United States. Italian Gewürz is the most underplayed. Some Gewürztraminers may be labelled simply Traminer.

The only possible taste confusion may be in Alsace with the grapey Muscat, as both grapes are very aromatic and have a sweet, flowery smell.

Defining the taste

Examine an Alsace Gewürztraminer from a recent vintage. Léon Beyer and Zind Humbrecht are renowned for their very rich Gewürz, Trimbach make a very crisp one, and Hugel are dependable. Note the curious perfume and try to come up with your own description of it: lychees, mangoes? Notice how it suggests sweetness on the nose but is then followed by a dry but very full-bodied taste. Try a bit on the tip of your tongue to test sweetness. Contrast the very powerful distinctive nose with that of a basic dry white table wine. Almost any other white wine will seem a very shy little flower indeed beside the orchidlike Gewürz. Seek out other examples of Gewürztraminer and note what they all have in common. Even light Gewürztraminers from Italy and New Zealand have that funny smell. Try to establish firmly your own palate picture of the varietal.

Comparing wines

If you get the chance, try a more advanced tasting—a Gewürztraminer alongside a Muscat. The most revealing pair would come from the same Alsace producer and should show similarities, but also the added richness, spice, and lesser grapiness that Gewürz has compared with the lighter Muscat.

Sauvignon and what sunshine does

Sauvignon Blanc is perhaps the second most distinctive grape variety and has great appeal for those who appreciate crisp, dry, uncomplicated wines.

Although its homeland is in the Loire appellations of Sancerre and Pouilly-Fumé, Sauvignon Blanc is grown in many wine regions around the world, including California and New Zealand, which is why I have chosen it to illustrate the effect of climate on taste.

Defining the taste

To get to grips with the essential Sauvignon-ness of Sauvignon Blanc you could not do better than start with a Sancerre or Pouilly-Fumé from a good grower. Vacheron and Bourgeois are both sound sources in Sancerre while Didier Dageneau and Ladoucette are two of the aristocrats of Pouilly-Fumé.

Try to establish your own trigger words for the grape. Green fruit? Herbaceous? Gooseberries? Grassy? Flinty? I find that a helpful way to recognize Sauvignon is first to realize that it hits your senses in a very direct way, so that it's "pointed" like a sword toward the middle of your mouth and nose rather than having a much broader fanlike flavor that approaches your senses in a cloud, like that of Gewürztraminer, or the Chardonnay grape examined below.

The distinctive smell

Sauvignon Blanc's chief attribute is its piercing, refreshing aroma. "Cats' pee on a gooseberry bush" may not sound a very appealing description to you, but after a bit of exposure to, and consideration of, the smell, you may come round to agreeing with this particular description of Sauvignon's distinctive smell. There's something very definitely "green" about it; some people find raw gooseberries, while others sense nettles, grass, or the smell of blackcurrant leaves (something rather akin to the smell of some less-ripe Cabernet Sauvignon, of which Sauvignon Blanc was recently proved to have been a parent). The very first whiff of this wine will immediately prepare you for the whack of acidity which will crinkle the edges of the tongue.

The loose but evocative adjective "flinty" is sometimes applied to Sauvignon, especially French Sauvignon. You are supposed to get a whiff of gunsmoke from a good Pouilly-Fumé and, indeed, as a ready victim of auto-suggestion, I often have, though I've never smelled actual gunsmoke. (This is what tasting notes are all about—finding terms that match flavors most closely and evocatively, even if only imagined.)

Climate and Sauvignon

The Loire valley is the coolest place where Sauvignon is cultivated, and Loire Sauvignons will usually be labeled with the name of one of the Sauvignon-producing appellations such as Sancerre, Pouilly-Fumé, Quincy, Reuilly, Menetou-Salon, or Touraine. Sauvignon de St. Bris, made in the far north of Burgundy, also demonstrates the cool climate style of Sauvignon that is dry, very acid, and almost steely, it's so pure and tart.

Sauvignon is also responsible for most dry white Bordeaux; the more temperate climate here in southwest France on the Atlantic seaboard can be tasted in the slightly less acidic, more open wines. Bordeaux Sauvignon is rarely as nervy and aromatic as Loire examples, and is often blended with the fatter Sémillon, (see page 108) Bordeaux's other popular white wine grape, to give more weight and a longer-lasting flavor. Without this palate-filler Sémillon, Bordeaux Sauvignon can be light to medium bodied.

The youthful wine

Sauvignon is a grape made for our impatient times. The wines should be drunk while they are young and fresh. Choose the youngest vintage available, for the grape's fruit is not the opulent sort that develops intriguing complexity with age. Instead, it simply gets a bit stale, sometimes a bit reminiscent of canned asparagus, and the initially high acidity starts to predominate. The wines are usually very pale straw in color, except in the rare (and expensive) examples that have been given a period in wood, and have taken on a golden tinge. Acidity is the most pronounced characteristic of the wines and almost all of them are fairly dry. There will rarely be any great length of flavor, which tends to tail off swiftly after a rather dashing start.

The New World

One New World wine region has staked its reputation on Sauvignon Blanc: Marlborough at the north of New Zealand's South Island. Cloudy Bay blazed the trail and a host of new labels have followed. The Sauvignons made here tend to have a more obvious, pungent fruitiness on the nose, a touch more apparent alcohol and often a little bit of sweetness to counteract the crystal-clear acidity that distinguishes New Zealand wines that are made so relatively far from the Equator.

SAUVIGNON BLANC VINES IN THE CLEAN AIR OF NEW ZEALAND.

New Zealand versus France

Compare a New Zealand, preferably Marlborough, Sauvignon Blanc such as Cloudy Bay or Brancott carrying the same year as your Sancerre/Pouilly-Fumé, or the one just after it (six months after the northern hemisphere harvest). The New World wine should have a much more powerful smell and its fruit and acidity are likely to taste more like separate components than in the more restrained French example. Compare the sweetness of the two wines; the French wine is likely to be drier and more minerally, less fruity. Many people prefer New Zealand Sauvignon Blanc to French, although a good French example (and there are many thin, weedy ones) is likely to improve after a year or two in the bottle whereas New Zealand wines can take on a rather tired asparagus note after a couple of years.

Around the world

The country producing Sauvignons that are most like New Zealand in style is Chile, with some quite elegant Sauvignon Blanc from the cool Casablanca Valley, thanks to careful study of New Zealand methods.

South Africa has a substantial acreage of Sauvignon Blanc and the wines such as Neil Ellis and Springfield Estate tend to taste like a quite delicate halfway house between France and New Zealand. Australia has few regions cool enough for appetizing Sauvignon Blanc, but the Adelaide Hills has reliable producers such as Shaw & Smith and Nepenthe.

The problem with Sauvignon Blanc in a warm climate is that it can rapidly lose its refreshing acidity and the zippy quality of the aroma. The Sauvignons of California, often oaked and called Fumé Blanc, show what happens when you transplant the variety to a positively warm climate. The nearer the Equator any sort of grapes are grown and ripened, the less acid and more sugar there will be in the resulting must, and the less acid and more alcohol there will be in the wine—unless deliberate steps are taken, such as picking the grapes unusually early, to counteract this natural phenomenon. A California Sauvignon Blanc will almost certainly have more alcohol and taste heavier than most French and New Zealand examples. There may also be some obvious oak, a little bit of oiliness from the Sémillon grape, which is sometimes blended in to provide a solid middle to the wine, and there will rarely be nearly as much leafy, green aroma since grassy herbaceousness is seen as a fault by so many American tasters. (Your first example of regional variations in wine style preferences.)

Compare and contrast
Compare a California Sauvignon—Mondavi Fumé Blanc is the gold standard, but any example would do—with your French and New Zealand examples. Note the increased body and reduced aroma of the California wine.

Of course, climate is only one of the many factors that affect the taste of wine. The differences you will taste in any range of Sauvignons could in part be attributed to things like their age, the age of the vines themselves, the winemaking techniques or even the exact clone of the vine planted. We will be examining all these factors, but at this point try to concentrate purely on the softening effect of sunshine. What has happened to the grapes can be tasted in the wine, whether it is a Sauvignon Blanc or, in fact, any other grape variety. The more acid a wine is, the less sunshine is likely to have ripened the grapes and the cooler the climate it is likely to have come from.

Chardonnay
and the kiss of oak

Chardonnay, a name virtually unknown thirty years ago when people drank Chablis and Chassagne rather than grapes, is today probably the best-known wine name of all.

From its homeland in Burgundy in eastern France it has migrated to virtually every spot on the globe where wine is produced. It has become so popular, and so widely planted that for many wine consumers white wine is Chardonnay. And yet, if you asked the millions of people who choose Chardonnay what it actually tastes like, I suspect very few of them would be able to provide an answer. For, unlike Sauvignon Blanc and Gewürztraminer, the Chardonnay grape itself does not have a particularly strong flavor or aroma. Perhaps that's why so many people like it.

We will see how the Chardonnay grape in different circumstances can produce wines with extremely varied characters, but Chardonnay is simply the slightly bland raw material fashioned by geographical circumstance (the local physical environment that the French call *terroir*) and/or the particular style of the winemaker.

Chardonnay is capable of a much wider range of styles and quality than either of the varieties examined so far. It can be lean and tart or extremely rich (if rarely downright sweet). It is usually still, but is also one of the classic ingredients in Champagne and other fizzy wines (see page 177). But Chardonnay is characterized by being dry, full-bodied and with a much "broader" flavor than the pointed, edgy Sauvignon. You can feel the weight of the wine immediately and know that this is no beguilingly aromatic aperitif, but a meaty, almost beefy, number that demands attention. Because of this weight and fullness, the acidity of a Chardonnay is not usually as noticeable as in the lighter-bodied Sauvignon. Chardonnay ripens relatively early and to relatively high alcohol levels, sometimes so high that the wine can taste deceptively sweet. Another very revealing characteristic of Chardonnay is that, unlike the two varietals studied so far, its flavor seems to gain intensity in the mouth. A seriously well-made example of this wine will have a fascinating long finish that may seem more powerful than the initial bouquet.

Defining the taste

To begin your voyage around Chardonnay, choose an inexpensive varietal bottling i.e. a wine labeled Chardonnay more obviously than on the basis of where it comes from. It could be a Vin de Pays d'Oc, an inexpensive Chardonnay carrying the simple appellation California, or one from that enormous grape sink known as Southeastern Australia (Lindemais Bin 65 is reliable). Try to choose one that makes no mention of oak or wood on the front or back label. Notice the blandness of the aroma relative to that of Sauvignon or Gewürztraminer. There should be nothing to object to in this wine, but little to seize upon either. Once you have a mouthful, notice how unlike water it tastes, how full bodied it is. Once you have swallowed it, see what a substantial impact it makes on the palate—arguably more than on the nose. You may notice a little sweetness, or a slightly hot sensation on the back of the palate. These are both signs of high alcohol.

To form your palate picture of Chardonnay you will need to taste more examples of it than were necessary to come to grips with the more obvious Gewürztraminer or Sauvignon Blanc grape—to begin with, ideally, all three examples suggested above. The following are all flavors that may be found in some unwooded Chardonnays: green apples, melons, butteriness, smokiness, hazelnuts, pineapple.

Barrels of flavor

One of the most famous marriages in the wine world is that between the Chardonnay grape and small oak barrels. It just seems as though they were made for each other—because oak, the winemaker's favorite sort of wood and its associated flavors, can supply much of that flavor that is missing from unadorned Chardonnay. A very high proportion of Chardonnay sold today has been made under the influence of oak in some way.

Chardonnay provides the best examples of how well wood and white wine can work together. A whole new range of flavors are introduced to make the wine much more complicated and rewarding, but they need time to meld together and produce a balanced wine. That's why wood aging makes most sense for wines destined for a longish life. There is not much point in giving

CHARDONNAY VINES IN MEURSAULT, ONE OF
BURGUNDY'S MOST FAMOUS WHITE WINE VILLAGES.

Sancerre a year in expensive small new oak casks as it is a wine that is made expressly to be enjoyed young and fresh—from the Sauvignon grape, which doesn't age particularly well.

Oak barrels are expensive and do much, much more than simply add oak flavor. They make the wine gentler and more sophisticated in texture as well as stabilizing and clarifying it naturally. However, there has been such a fashion for oak flavor that many wine producers, wishing to offer oak flavor without the expense and inconvenience of demanding oak barrels, choose to use much cheaper, easier oak chips or oak staves instead. These are typically suspended in a stainless steel tank during fermentation when the wine is most likely to absorb flavor. If a label claims that a wine is oaked or wooded without mentioning barrels specifically, and is relatively inexpensive, then it will probably have been made this way. Such wines are fine if you drink them young, but such an artificial way of adding oak flavor has only short-term effects and the wines can turn nasty and oily after just a year or two.

The next stage is to taste a Chardonnay that has benefited from all the advantages of a small new oak barrel, typically about fifty gallons (225 liters) capacity. (The smaller and newer the barrel, the more oak flavor elements it has to impart. You can achieve the textural advantages without much oak flavor by using older barrels.) The classic way of making good Chardonnay in its homeland Burgundy is to ferment the wine in such barrels, then leave the wine sitting on some of the sediment, or lees, of that first, alcoholic fermentation, every now and then stirring those lees to add extra flavor and character to the wine, to avoid the formation of hydrogen sulfide (see pages 38–39) and to draw certain elements such as pigment and astringent compounds out of the wine.

The wine is also encouraged to go through another, second fermentation in the barrel, known as the malolactic fermentation, or MLF, so-called because it transforms harsh malic, green-appley acid to softer, milky lactic acid. This technique, originating in Burgundy, is now widely applied around the world by any even remotely ambitious Chardonnay producer, resulting in remarkable uniformity among "BFC's" (barrel-fermented Chardonnays) virtually everywhere.

Chips, not barrels

Try to track down one of these inexpensive "oaked" or "wooded" Chardonnays. You will need to read the labels carefully (see page 99). A Chardonnay that has been carelessly chipped (made with oak chips) tastes a little like sawdust when young, and heavy and oily at two years old. Bulgaria has been a great exponent of oak chips, but commercial producers in practically every wine-producing country in the world—with the possible exception of oak-free Germany—have used them.

The real thing

Taste a proper, barrel-fermented Chardonnay made virtually anywhere except Burgundy. A good example would be any mid- to high-priced offering from California, where this technique is well established. Notice the relatively pale color (barrel fermentation encourages coloring matter to settle out of the wine). Notice too the smooth creaminess of the texture (astringent elements are also settled out of the wine during this process). Look for a certain milky or even buttery element on the nose; this is a characteristic of malolactic fermentation (although in truly fine wine it should not be obvious). Now, how about the oak? Monitor whether you can actually smell any oak flavor, or sense any astringency or bitterness on the palate.

Oak, the backlash

The presence, or lack of any oakiness is currently one of the most contentious issues for wine in general and Chardonnay in particular. In the 1980s wine consumers were intrigued by this very obvious new flavor element, and wine producers exhibited an extremely varied range of skills at handling the latest wine-making toy that was oak. Sometimes, in newer wine regions in particular, wines that were fermented in neutral stainless steel were then put into new oak barrels, bursting with their own flavors and tannins, without giving the wines a chance to drop all those astringent elements and coloring matter. The result was some very odd, imbalanced wines that had gained nothing in texture and tended to go brown and coarse after only a year or two in bottle.

Every action is inevitably followed by a reaction—in this case, horror in some quarters at any obvious oak elements in a wine at all (even though consumers still value the textural benefits of barrel fermentation in their Chardonnays). In Australia, where oakiness had admittedly reached its limits in white wines, this even resulted in a trend for Chardonnays which proudly proclaimed their

USED BARRELS STACKED AT CHÂTEAU BONNET, ENTRE-DEUX-MERS, BORDEAUX.

CHARDONNAY GRAPES IN CHABLIS WHERE
THE WINE RARELY TASTES OF OAK.

Unoaked or Unwooded status on the label (sometimes even commanding a premium!).

My own view is that in a top-quality young barrel-fermented Chardonnay, a hint of the expensive oak to which it has been treated is not necessarily a fault (just as a slightly high tannin level is expected of a fine young red wine), but the oak has to taste good. It may exhibit the warm vanilla toastiness of American oak, or the more focused, tight-knit savory quality of well-seasoned French oak, but too sweet, charred, or toasty and it can be intrusive. Too green or astringent and the wood probably has not been seasoned well or long enough. Having said that, what California's most famous wine man Robert Mondavi used to call "a kiss of oak" is no bad thing in a young wine and will mature, by marrying with all the other flavor elements in the wine, into something even more complex and interesting.

For, unlike Sauvignon Blanc and Gewürztraminer, top-quality Chardonnay is designed to mature in the bottle. Generally speaking, you find that the riper the grapes, or the higher yield of the vines that produced them, the shorter the life of the Chardonnay in bottle and vice versa.

Regional differences

Chardonnay's home is eastern France in general and Burgundy in particular (in fact DNA testing has shown that its parents are the ancient Pinot vine and an obscure and equally ancient light-berried vine called Gouais Blanc). Not all white Burgundy is great, but the majority of great Chardonnay comes from Burgundy. What makes this region special as a wine producer is the varied range of styles and flavors of wine it can produce, depending on the exact area, or appellation, in which it is made. And it is these dozens of different appellations, rather than the word Chardonnay itself, that appear on the label. To enjoy white Burgundy therefore, you have to learn a little geography.

The coolest part of Burgundy is Chablis in the far north of France, where virtually nothing but Chardonnay is planted and where traditionally oak use and influence has been minimal. True Chablis is a uniquely lean, green form of Chardonnay that, because in most years the grapes have to struggle to ripen, needs and repays years of maturing in the bottle. I have tasted forty-year-old Chablis that was still getting better. Chablis' typical maturation pattern is quite unlike that of any other Chardonnay, partly because of the initial high acidity but also probably because of its unique soil type (Kimmeridgean to be precise). When it is young, it tastes almost Sauvignonlike in its appetizing, piercingly high acid form, although it is much more likely to smell of cool, damp stones (I know it sounds ridiculous) than green fruits or grass. In its middle age, around five or six years old, it can go through a rather offputting stage reminiscent of wet wool, but then it climbs out of this to glorious maturity. At this stage, it is still extremely racy and steely with its high acidity but has gained a much more complicated and rewarding bouquet that has a dense, intriguing quality that I describe as "mealy"—a bit like oatmeal. For Chablis that will age well, it is best to head for one that is labeled Premier Cru ("first growth"—growth as in plot of land) or, even better, Grand Cru ("great growth").

Chardonnay prices start to get serious quite a way south of Chablis on the Côte d'Or, the narrow "golden slope" that is the heartland of the Burgundy region. These wines qualify as Grands

Crus and include Corton-Charlemagne, Le Montrachet, Bâtard-Montrachet, Chevalier-Montrachet, and some Premier Cru Meursaults—all of which are extremely full bodied yet subtle and, above all, savory. They tend to exhibit a whole range of flavors, including hazelnuts, licorice as well as minerals of all sorts.

Top Côte d'Or producers tend to use a mixture of new and used oak for their best Chardonnays (depending on the characteristics of the vintage years) but the aim is to keep the oak flavor restrained and in harmony with the fruit. This is the ideal to which producers of Chardonnay all over the world aspire and some of them, particularly top Californian producers such as those cited below, show every sign of beating the Burgundians at their own game.

The distinctions between the wines of Burgundy's famous white wine villages can therefore easily be blurred by the different winemaking regimes of different producers, but if we want to talk in stereotypes, Meursault is buttery, Puligny-Montrachet is steely and creamy, while next door Chassagne-Montrachet can be slightly nuttier and more textured. All of the white Burgundies named above are designed to be aged. In fact, it is a waste of (a lot of) money to open a Grand Cru Burgundy before its fifth or sixth birthday and a Premier Cru before its third or fourth. And even a village Meursault (one that simply has the name of the village on the label instead of any specific vineyard) from a great producer such as Comtes Lafon or Coche-Dury may continue to improve in the bottle for up to five years in a very good vintage.

Not quite as great, but still good, white Burgundies can be found lurking behind labels saying Pernand-Vergelesses, Auxey-Duresses, St. Aubin, Rully, Montagny, and Bourgogne Blanc, all of whose wines tend to be lighter and a bit leaner. From the southern, less smart, end of Burgundy, almost as far south as Beaujolais, come Chardonnays called St. Véran, Pouillys of all sorts except Pouilly-Fumé, Beaujolais Blanc, and Mâcon Blanc. These wines are for much earlier drinking when they can be attractively plump and welcoming, reminiscent of apples or melons, and only rarely show much oak influence.

Lean, green Chablis

Taste a Chablis, ideally one that is
two or three years old (notice how
much more youthful it tastes than
a Chardonnay of this age from a
warmer region) and also one that
is much older. (I hope for your sake
it has passed the wet wool stage
and reached the mealy stage.)
Chablis is a minority taste in
this oak-obsessed age (and an
increasing number of Chablis
producers now use some new oak)
so it may be difficult to track down
a mature example outside a
serious restaurant. You may just
have to do the aging yourself, but
be consoled by the fact that
Chablis is much the best value of
great white Burgundy.

If you want to taste Chardonnay
in an even less ripe form, track
down a still wine made in the
Champagne region, sold as a

Coteaux Champenois Blanc de
Blancs. Its extreme leanness
provides the perfect explanation of
why Champagne specializes in
sparkling and not still wines.

Expensive Burgundy

Try to get your hands on and your
tasting equipment wrapped around
as many different examples of
white Burgundy as possible. Any
comparison between a simpler
example such as any cited in the
paragraph on page 104 on good
but not great Burgundies and a
more expensive one from one of
the three great white wine villages
Puligny-Montrachet, Chassagne-
Montrachet, and Meursault should
be very instructive. The latter
should be much weightier and, in
youth, more reserved, longer
lasting in the glass—or at least in
the opened bottle.

New World Chardonnay

Chardonnay has been an enormous success in California and
Australia and they are winding themselves up to a similar peak in
South Africa and New Zealand. It has become all the rage in Italy
now and there are also plantings from Catalonia to Lebanon, from
Chile to New York State.

Australian Chardonnay is particularly distinctive. It has a sort
of "twang" to the nose which is definitively citrus, closest in relation
to lime, and it often has a very slight greenish tinge to its deep gold.
The Australians are past masters at delivering reliably made
Chardonnay bargains since they began producing enough grapes.
And the fact that they were the first to use oak chips to imbue
cheaper wines with some oaky flavor means that they also now use

them more subtly than, say, typical Eastern European wine producers. Any Chardonnay that simply says Southeastern Australia on the label rather than specifying a particular region (such as the particularly successful, for Chardonnay, Adelaide Hills or Margaret River, for example) is probably made from blended fruit from the vast irrigated wine regions of Australia's interior. Such wines can be great bargains but don't bother to age them. Most of these

MONTANA'S SUPREMELY
PHOTOGENIC BRANCOTT ESTATE IN
MARLBOROUGH, NEW ZEALAND.

wines should be drunk as early as you possibly can, but examples such as Giaconda, Petaluma Tiers Vineyard, and Leeuwin prove that Australians can also make Chardonnays with real finesse and aging potential.

Chardonnay is also the most planted grape in New Zealand, and the trademark of the typical New Zealand Chardonnay is the streak of clean, green acidity. South Africa's Chardonnays can be attractively smokey, while Chilean Chardonnays taste like the inexpensive, sometimes almost watery copies of North American Chardonnay that they, in fact, are.

California's Chardonnays are extremely varied: from the rich intensity of the best quality down to heavy, sweet liquid without very much character apart from that of alcohol. Some of the best Chardonnays tend to come from Carneros, parts of Sonoma (especially the emerging Sonoma Coast vineyards) and the Central Coast, but there always exceptions. Some of the most reliable names to look for (although the best are in short supply) are Marcassin, Kistler, Au Bon Climat, Talley, Flowers, and the Reserve Chardonnays of Robert Mondavi.

Oak and climate

By looking carefully at the wide range of different styles of Chardonnay available today, no matter where they come from, you should get a good idea of the extra richness in color, body, and flavor that oak gives to a white wine. You will also have reinforced the lessons already learned about the influence of climate on wine. Contrast, for example, Chardonnays from California and Canada, or the Finger Lakes. They will have been made almost identically; that distinctive clean green acidity in the latter example is simply the work of nature—being much further from the Equator and therefore cooler.

Chardonnay is grown in virtually every wine region elsewhere, but rarely shows much local character. Of all the wine styles made today, barrel-fermented Chardonnay is the most "international," with all the connotations of a loss of local identity that that word entails. At its worst, Chardonnay is a bland alcoholic drink that forms a useful halfway house between soft drinks and wine; at its best, an expression of *terroir*, power, and potential.

Sémillon—a great rotter

*Sémillon, usually spelled Semillon outside France, is not as well
known as it deserves to be. Even members of the dwindling ranks of
Sauternes lovers are often unaware of the crucial role played by this
particular vine variety in its production.*

No serious wine drinker would ever confess ignorance of, or
aversion to, Chardonnay, but such is the Cinderella-like state in
which this grape languishes that the word Sémillon is relatively
rarely found on a wine label. It is, nevertheless, slowly becoming
more popular with wine producers at least (if not necessarily
consumers) as providing another string to a bow usually dominated
by Chardonnay and Sauvignon Blanc.

Grown in Washington state (where it was pioneered by
L'Ecole No. 41), in South Africa (where Stellenzicht has produced
some of the finest), it is also increasingly respected in New Zealand,
where the organic Millton Vineyard has managed to make serious,
sometimes sweet examples.

It has traditionally been used to blend with the much leaner
and more aromatic Sauvignon Blanc, particularly but not
exclusively in Bordeaux and the rest of southwest France. (This is a
common practice in the southern hemisphere, too.) In fact, less-
than-fully-ripe Sémillon can smell remarkably like Sauvignon Blanc
(just as that Bordeaux red grape Cabernet Sauvignon, when less
than fully ripe, can smell like Cabernet Franc). These two grapes are
clearly made for each other.

Only in Australia, and especially in the Hunter Valley, has
Semillon (l's pronounced and no accent) a long tradition of being
taken seriously as a varietal, to be vinified by itself as a dry white
worthy of aging and labeling as Semillon. Youthful Australian
Semillons provide a relatively rare opportunity to taste the grape
unblended with its habitual Bordeaux partner Sauvignon.

Sémillon is relatively low in acid, even weightier and more
alcoholic than Chardonnay, and hence carries with it the suggestion
of sweetness even when it is vinified dry. Some tasters find figs in its
flavors, others cigars. It can have a definite edge of citrus as well and
there is something almost waxy, that veers to oily in very ripe
examples, in its texture. Clues to the grape's identity are a deep
golden color, lots of alcohol, and low acidity.

As Sémillon ages it takes on an almost orange color whether it is a dry or sweet wine, and the mature dry Semillons of the Hunter Valley are some of the wine world's most curious and underappreciated treasures. They are, it must be said, an acquired taste. The wines seem to lose their early message of the grape and take on the character of the land itself. Any Hunter wine more than a decade old starts to display a curious minerally taste which I call a "volcanic twang" and has been called "burnt toast." This applies to every variety cultivated there, and is one of the most striking examples I have come across to support the traditional European view that the actual composition of the soil and subsoil in any region determines the flavor of wine. (The more modern view is that it is soil texture rather than soil composition that is important, i.e. that the land is well drained enough to encourage deep roots seeking moisture and therefore a complex root system.) There is a high proportion of volcanic soil in the best bit of the Hunter, just as there is in Madeira—this may account for my "twang."

HUNTER VALLEY SEMILLON IN NEW SOUTH WALES — BECOMING ALL TOO RARE.

Defining the taste

To see what the grape itself tastes like, try to track down a youthful Semillon from Australia, or another example unblended with Sauvignon Blanc. Notice, even on a fairly young example, that this wine has a low acidity and yellowish color, with hints of the spiciness to come. Roll it round the mouth to feel the full weight of the wine. You might even note a certain creaminess of texture with the smoothness of lanolin. Semillon, like Chardonnay, is not searingly aromatic and, with its relatively heavy body, it lumbers toward you rather than attacking you with a point of sharp flavor.

Hunter Valley and the "volcanic twang"

Try to get hold of a mature example of Australian Semillon, ideally but not necessarily from the Hunter Valley. Notice—in fact you won't be able to avoid it—the curiousness of the old Semillon's flavor, as well as its deep color and weight. That is my volcanic twang: a taste almost of burnt earth, with lots of mineral trace elements close to the surface. There is something reminiscent of the black charcoal biscuits served in the gentlemen's clubs in London, England—though I appreciate that few readers of this book may know what I'm on about.

Blending and botrytis

To experience Sémillon's greatest contribution to wine pleasure, however, it is necessary to look at sweet white Bordeaux, especially the best wines from the communes of Sauternes and Barsac. We have already touched on the Bordeaux recipe of blending Sauvignon Blanc with the richness of Sémillon for its fuller-bodied dry white wines such as in Graves and Pessac-Léognan. Just down the road in Sauternes, Barsac and Bordeaux's less famous sweet wine districts, a bit of Sauvignon is often added to Sémillon to give the resultant blend a bit of extra acidity while keeping it predominantly Sémillon and sweet.

To make a great sweet wine you must have grapes that contain an awful lot of sugar, so that even when you have fermented enough to produce the wine's alcohol content you are still left with lots of fruity richness. The best sweet white wines in the world share a common helper toward this gloriously luscious state, in the form of a rather unsavory-looking mould called *botrytis cinerea*, or "noble rot." In certain propitious autumnal conditions (damp mornings followed

ROTTING CHENIN BLANC (LEFT) AND RIESLING (RIGHT) GRAPES IN VOUVRAY AND THE RHEINGAU RESPECTIVELY.

by warm, sunny afternoons), this attacks the grapes and—without breaking them and causing spoilage—shrivels them to concentrate their sugar content. Botrytis gives a special honeyed vegetal quality to the taste of overripe grapes and imbues the wines with sometimes extraordinary aging capacity (I have tasted an 1811 Sauternes that was in the peak of condition). It occurs only in vintages when conditions are just right, and only in certain places. For years, California's vine growers tried to eliminate grapes affected by this nasty-looking mold because they didn't realize what lovely things it could do for grapes such as Riesling, Gewürztraminer, and Sémillon. Vintages that are too dry can produce sweet wines, but they won't have the curious whiff of botrytis—to which Sémillon, with its thin skin, is conveniently prone.

The sweet taste of botrytis

You could at this stage see whether you can detect the difference in taste between a botrytized, carefully oaked sweet white Bordeaux and an ordinary one. To see what all the fuss is about, compare a classed growth Sauternes (which will be expensive) with the cheapest sweet white wine from Bordeaux you can find—perhaps a Ste. Croix du Mont or Loupiac, or even a cheap Monbazillac from the Bergerac region east of Bordeaux. Ideally the Sauternes should carry the vintage year in which there was considerable benevolent botrytis effect such as 1999, 1998, or 1997 or, if you are feeling extremely rich, 1990, 1989, or 1988. Note how much sugarier, oilier, and less appetizing the cheaper wine is— and how in the Sauternes, the high level of sweetness is balanced by an intensity of flavor and lots of acidity so that, unlike the cheap wine, it is not at all sickly.

Riesling—
the greatest white wine grape

Poor old Riesling, the most underappreciated (and mispronounced) white grape in the world, but in my opinion the finest.

theory

Its reputation has been horribly sullied by two facts. Firstly, it is irrevocably associated with Germany, whose most cynical merchants have exported so much extremely disappointing wine—nay sugarwater—that the reputation of even the best German wines (most of which are made from Riesling) has suffered.

Secondly, the name Riesling has been appropriated in various countries for other, usually much less noble grapes. In Australia and South Africa, for example, a very ordinary grape whose proper name is Crouchen was for long called Clare Riesling and Cape or Paarl Riesling respectively. Throughout Eastern Europe is a grape which has been known variously as Italian Riesling, Riesling Italico, Welschriesling, Laski Rizling, Olasz Rizling, and many similar aliases. Probably the first wine of which I was conscious was served to my grandmother and me at a sedate Somerset luncheon party in the late 1960s, and we called it Lutomer Rize-ling. We were wrong on two counts. We should have pronounced the word Riesling "reece-ling" of course and, furthermore, the wine wasn't "proper" Riesling but the imposter, Laski Rizling. This other variety—let's call it Welschriesling—can make some pretty good wine, especially sweet wine in Austria, but a high proportion of it that has reached export markets from eastern Europe has been pretty ropey stuff which has done nothing for the reputation of the (completely unrelated) great Riesling of Germany.

The only characteristic that this Welschriesling has in common with the noble Riesling of Germany (sometimes called Rhine Riesling, Rheinriesling, Riesling Renano, Rajinskirizling, and Johannisberg Riesling outside Germany) is that it tends to make slightly perfumed, medium dry wines with a fair bit of acidity.

Real Riesling is a much more finicky vine. If planted too close to the Equator, it ripens so fast that the wine has no interesting flavor at all. When it is as far from the Equator as Germany, where it reaches its apogee, it needs a well-favored site to stand a chance of ripening (unlike the much earlier-ripening grapes that less quality-conscious German producers grow such as Müller Thurgau). The vast proportion (95 percent) of Germany's fine wine is made from Riesling, which, like Chardonnay, has been planted in many regions around the world by winemakers aspiring to the exciting race and breed of the prototypes.

The twin hallmarks of Riesling's great quality as a white wine grape are its exceptional ability to communicate *terroir* (the characteristics specific to the particular vineyard in which it was grown) and, more than even top-quality Chardonnay, its beautiful evolution with age. In fact, it matures at a very similar rate to that long-ager, red Bordeaux from the Médoc.

Just like mature Chardonnay and Sémillon, an aged Riesling takes on a more intense color, often a deep gold but in this case with a greenish tinge. The bouquet evolves after years in the bottle into something much more layered than the simple floweriness of young

PIESPORT IN THE MOSEL WHERE GREAT RIESLING IS MADE (EVEN IF ITS NAME IS, CONFUSINGLY, BORROWED FOR SO MUCH DREARY PIESPORTER MICHELSBERG).

Riesling. It is faintly reminiscent of gasoline, though still enticing and extremely pure in its appeal. A Riesling is often steely, but fruity acidity is its most obvious distinguishing mark. As the Riesling ages, this acidity becomes more apparent while the sweetness seems to recede. After many years in bottle, the wine seems to taste dry and too tart.

Defining the taste

Compare a basic cheap Liebfraumilch or Niersteiner Gutes Domtal with a bottle of serious German wine, one with the word Riesling on the label and which costs at least twice and preferably three times the price of the former. Notice how like water the cheaper wine tastes. Does the cheaper wine have anything like the flavor and intensity of the Riesling? Which wine is more interesting?

Try to find a German Riesling that is at least five years old. This should not be too expensive as demand for German wines is, alas, not that great and the wines tend to sell far slower than they should. Don't worry about anything that looks like white crystals in the bottle. These will not be at all harmful (see page 43). Notice how the color of the wine has deepened from the very pale greenish straw of a young wine to something a little more golden. Then smell the wine. It should have a very distinctive bouquet which will, of course, depend on how good the wine was to begin with.

A very fine German wine will have as many layers of flavor as a great red Bordeaux but, as it nears the end of its active life, it will often have an aroma suggestive of gasoline or kerosene with, often, layers of mineral notes. Excellent producers of a German Riesling include Loosen, Egon Müller, J. J. Prüm, von Schubert and Robert Weil.

Acid and alcohol

It may change considerably with age, but even in its early life Riesling is marked by very zesty acid, relatively low alcohol (say 8 to 11 percent compared to the more alcoholic Chardonnay's range of 12 to 14 percent) and a delicate flowery fruit aroma which shouts refreshment to the senses. With this refreshing acidity and lowish alcohol, Riesling can be a much more appetizing aperitif, even when it has a certain amount of fruity sweetness, than fuller-bodied wines such as most Chardonnays—and it can also be extremely food-friendly.

Within Germany itself there is great interest in the new wave of trocken (dry) and halbtrocken (half-dry) wines, which go even better with food than the more commonly exported German wines which, typically, have had some perceptible fruity sweetness.

Chardonnay and Riesling

Compare a typical Chardonnay with a typical Riesling and notice that although both may seem to have a certain amount of sweetness (from alcohol and grape sugar respectively), and the Riesling may have considerable "extract" (mineral elements to add flavor), the Riesling is much lighter in alcohol and higher in acidity.

Try to find a German wine labeled "trocken" or "halbtrocken" and see for yourself whether you prefer your German Rieslings dry or whether you like the acidity to be counterbalanced by a bit of fruitiness. Try both styles of wine with food, too.

Riesling around the world

In the world of wine, as in every other, what we have least of is what we want most. The winemaker in southern Italy or California tries desperately to keep the acidity level in his wines up under the powerful glare of the ripening sun. His counterpart at the northern limit of German vine cultivation lusts after more sunshine to ripen his grapes, and the most prized German wines are those highest in natural sugar. Only in the sunniest vintages is much sweet wine made there. But Riesling Beerenauslesen (BA), and Trockenbeerenauslesen (TBA), which are picked very late to trap every last ray of sunshine in the bottle, can provide more good examples of botrytis, called Edelfäule—at a price.

The very sweet Rieslings, TBAs and BAs, are usually fiendishly expensive. Curiously, however, wines that are only medium dry to medium sweet, Spätlesen and Auslesen, or an even more delicate, usually drier, Kabinett can often be good value—especially if they have aged at all, as standard German pricing practice seems to have ignored inflation. Such wines can provide wonderful examples of what happens to Riesling as it ages.

RIESLING GRAPES IN ALSACE ABSORBING EVERY RAY OF AUTUMN SUNLIGHT.

The effect of climate on taste is well illustrated even within the fairly close wine regions of Germany. German wine is sold either in green or brown bottles, the green ones coming from the Mosel and its tributaries, the Saar and Ruwer, and the brown from Rhine river regions such as the Rheingau, Rheinhessen, and Pfalz. Because they are even cooler than Rhine vineyards, those on the steep slopes of the Mosel produce lighter, crisper wines. Some of them may have only about 7 percent alcohol, while those of the Rhine are at least one degree stronger and taste noticeably more substantial. Traveling upriver past the Rheingau to Rheinhessen and Pfalz, one encounters increasingly full-bodied wines that have gained intensity and ripeness with more sunshine.

Riesling is the most respected wine cultivated in Alsace just across the Rhine from Germany's most southerly wine region Baden, cheek by jowl with the rather richer Gewürztraminer grape. It should be easy to distinguish an Alsace Riesling (which in some ways gives a particularly clear picture of the aroma of the Riesling grape) from most German wines because Alsace winemakers ferment all the sugar out to make dry, even aggressively bone dry, wines. They still have the perfumed floweriness on the nose, but are dry on the palate. Trimbach's Clos Ste. Hune is one of the finest.

Another stronghold of Riesling in Europe is the Wachau Kremstal region of Austria, which produces some of the finest examples in the world, combining the dryness of Alsace with the fragrance and transparency of the best of Germany. Those labeled Smaragd are the richest, and in very ripe vintages such as 1998 can taste positively sweet as well as very alcoholic. These wines can be difficult to find but are undoubtedly noble.

theory

Riesling, often labeled Rhine Riesling there, is widely planted in Australia, especially South Australia where there was a wave of immigration from Silesia in the last century. The two most famous areas for Riesling are the Eden Valley and Clare Valley. Being from southern hemisphere vineyards that are harvested in February and March, such a vintage-dated wine always has a good six months' greater age than European equivalents. Moreover, Australian Rhine Rieslings age more rapidly than their German counterparts. Even after as little as three years, they can be deep yellow and busy giving off all sorts of interesting gasoline-like signs of age. Cheaper examples of Rhine Rieslings can have a slightly sickly smell, but you will find that the better examples such as those of Petaluma, Grosset, Knappstein, Pike's, and Mount Langi Ghiran are different altogether. These particular examples have real nerve as well as body and make fantastic partners for spicy food. Some of the best wines of New York's Finger Lakes region and Canada's Ontario are steely Rieslings.

Non-German Riesling

Compare an Alsace Riesling with a German one of the same vintage. Notice how much less alcohol the German wine has (Alsace winemakers routinely add sugar during fermentation to make their wines stronger.) And how much drier and steelier the Alsace wine seems. Try to identify what they have in common, for this is the essential Riesling-ness of Riesling.

Now compare an Australian Riesling. Notice how much more full-bodied—and food-friendly?—it is than a sweeter German example.

In the late 1970s and 1980s, California also had unexpected success with the grape they call the Johannisberg Riesling, or JR— particularly with very sweet counterparts to BA or TBA wines, usually called Special Late Harvest or Special Select Late Harvest. The wines have much more body and alcohol than their German counterparts, and they age much, much faster, but careful winemakers kept acidity levels well up. Alas, Riesling and sweet wines have been so deeply unfashionable in California that the acreage devoted to this noble grape has dwindled considerably. Washington and Oregon to the north have had slightly more success with their leaner, smokier style of Riesling, however.

Chenin blanc
and the importance of yield

*The Chenin Blanc grape is another undervalued grape, and is
unusual in that it is grown extensively throughout the world's wine
regions, with enormous variation in the taste of the wine it produces.
It makes fairly ordinary wines in the main, but the best examples
can continue to improve in bottle for decades.*

The home of the Chenin Blanc is the Loire valley and, in particular,
the long middle stretch upriver from Muscadet country toward the
distant vineyards of Sancerre and Pouilly-Fumé. It is the basic grape
of Anjou Blanc, Saumur (still and sparkling), and Vouvray and
Montlouis (still, sparkling, sweet, and dry). Even within the confines
of the tiny appellation Vouvray, the versatility of the Chenin Blanc
grape is amply demonstrated. In this appellation it makes wines of
all degrees of sweetness, fizziness, and potential. Basic Loire Chenin
Blanc has a faint honey-and-flowers smell, with far-from-unpleasant
hints of damp straw. Like any Loire wine, these basic Chenins have
lots and lots of acidity—remember how Loire Sauvignons taste (see
page 94)?

There are little pockets of vineyards on the Loire, however,
where the Chenin Blanc can produce honeyed wines that can last,
if not forever, then certainly for half as long. When they are young,
they have so much acidity that it is difficult to believe they have
much sweetness in them at all. But, as they mature, they develop a
lovely, round, almost "gummy" character that takes them closer to
the golden syrup mold. Wines such as Vouvray and Montlouis are
usually made in a wide range of degrees of richness, from *sec* (dry),
through *demi-sec* (medium dry) to *moelleux* (sweet). After a decade
or two the color of the wine takes on a wonderful golden luster, but
the key to a Loire Chenin Blanc, however old and however sweet, is
very high acidity together with some honey and a suggestion of
summer flowers.

Chenin Blanc is grown widely in California and South Africa
(where it is by far the most commonly planted grape) and also in
Australia and South America. What is extraordinary is how unlike
Loire Chenins these wines taste. Standard California Chenin Blanc
is pretty neutral, off dry, grown mainly in the Central Valley on very

high-yielding vines, and is used for straightforward, medium dry inexpensive wines that provide a good base for the winemaker's skill. South African Chenin Blancs are different again, with a bit more acidity to them, (often) a tiny bit of gas but rarely any hint of the rich character of a Loire Chenin.

theory

practice

Defining the taste

To experience plain, unadorned Loire Chenin Blanc, try any white wine labeled Anjou, Saumur, or Vouvray. Notice the fruity, appetizing nature of the wine. There is lots of acidity and some honeyed, almost peachy flavor but noticeably more body and "breadth" than the Riesling grape would give. Palpably better quality, and often ludicrously underpriced, are the wines of Coteaux du Layon, Quarts de Chaume, Bonnezeaux, and those of quality-conscious Vouvray producers such as Gaston Huet, Fouquet, A. Foreau, and Marc Brédif. These are wines with real honey (especially if, as in some Bonnezeaux, Quarts de Chaume and Vouvray in 1997, botrytis has

struck) as well as a gold color. Acidity will always be high but the richness of the wines gradually builds up over the years. I have never tasted a Loire wine of this type that seemed over the hill—and I have tasted several wines from the 1920s.

Compare your Loire Chenin Blanc example with one from South Africa. They hardly taste as though they are made from the same grape, do they? There is so much less flavor and intensity in the Cape example. To maximize the amount of flavor in your South African Chenin, choose one that boasts of having been made from "bush vines"—vines that have been grown without wires and are therefore usually lower in yield.

Part of the explanation for these wide variations may be that different clones of the Chenin Blanc variety have been developed in these different areas, but one indubitable factor is the question of yields. In very general terms, if a vine is asked to bear too much fruit, that fruit will lack flavor and character compared with a vine grown in exactly the same conditions that has been more severely pruned. Average yields in South African and Californian Chenin Blanc are considerably higher than the Loire valley average, which probably helps to explain just how vapid so many of these New World examples taste.

CHENIN BLANC AND THE IMPORTANCE OF YIELD   119

Rhône whites—
increasingly fashionable

Just as the red wine grapes of the Rhône Valley in southeast France have become extremely fashionable, so have their white counterparts.

VIOGNIER VINES IN CONDRIEU, ON SLOPES SO STEEP THEY HAVE TO BE TERRACED.

The most fashionable of all is Viognier, the headily perfumed grape of the Condrieu appellation on the right bank of the river, just south of Lyons. Now widely planted in the Languedoc in southern France, in parts of California and increasingly in Australia and Italy, it produces wines that are typically very full bodied with a scent almost as distinctive and powerful as that of Gewürztraminer. Apricots, both dried and fresh, and May blossom are all words that are commonly used to describe it.

The nerviest, most elegant white Rhône grape is Roussanne, which is traditionally associated with white Hermitage but is now planted all over southern France. It is also quite full bodied, but is usually distinguished by a green, lime-blossom acidity and flavors that are reminiscent of greengages. Roussanne's classic blending partner is Marsanne, which is a much broader sort of grape that often lacks acidity and can taste remarkably like marzipan— particularly in its Australian versions—although it too is widely planted in southern France.

Defining the taste

Specimens of Viognier are increasingly easy to find. Condrieu and Château Grillet are the only appellations which demand this grape exclusively, but look for varietal examples from Languedoc, California, even Australia and South Africa. Fairview's South African and Fetzer's Californian Viogniers are model specimens at a much lower price than any Condrieu. Great Condrieu producers include Cuilleron, Gangloff, Niero, Villard, Guigal, and Delas.

Roussanne and Marsanne

Try to find varietal examples of these two white North Rhône grapes; California's Central Coast and southern France are the most likely hunting grounds (the first great varietal Roussanne to have come my way was Ch de Beaucastel's special oaked cuvée from Châteauneuf) although there are considerable plantings of Marsanne in the Australian state of Victoria. Likely California producers include Alban, Bonny Doon, and Andrew Murray. Tahbilk and Michelton specialize in Australian Marsanne while Aeolia is the finest varietal Roussanne down under.

Other grapes

Grenache Blanc, the pale-skinned version of the southern Rhône red grape Grenache, is less noble than these two—in fact, it can be downright blowsy, so full bodied are most examples. As a blending partner, it can add body and is most commonly encountered in the south of France and, as Garnacha Blanca, in some white Riojas.

Rolle/Vermentino are the French/Italian names for a lively grape planted particularly in Languedoc-Roussillon and Sardinia.

The white Pinot family

Chardonnay has many cousins, of which two carry the first name of their common parent Pinot Noir.

Pinot Blanc, known as Pinot Bianco in northeast Italy, which grows lots of it, and Weissburgunder in German-speaking countries, does indeed taste a bit like a timid cousin of the flamboyant Chardonnay. It has the same sort of broad flavor and smudgy, indistinct perfume with perhaps a little more smokiness.

Pinot Gris, Italy's popular Pinot Grigio, has positively pink skin, which often releases some pigments into the wine so that it is characteristically a deep golden color and, often, quite alcoholic and rich—much more so in Alsace, the French home of these two French Pinots, than in northeast Italy. Oregon has made a speciality of Pinot Gris. Look especially for Cristom and Willa Kenzie.

Defining the taste

Compare a Pinot Blanc and Pinot Gris from the same producer and, preferably, vintage. Alsace could provide many examples, as could Friuli in northeast Italy. The Pinot Gris—or Pinot Grigio—should have noticeably more weight, a deeper color (thanks to those pink skins) and a more exotic perfume. The Pinot Blanc, on the other hand, is like a pale Chardonnay.

A third cousin of Chardonnay is Melon, the rather neutral grape that is solely responsible for the almost salty wines of Muscadet at the mouth of the river Loire.

Some local specialities

Albariño

The finest grape of the wet, green Galicia region in northwest Spain, it is becoming increasingly popular. It makes racy, lemon-perfumed wines with a real backbone and is also valued, as Alvarinho, as the most noble grape for Vinho Verde just across the border in northern Portugal.

Grüner Veltliner

Austria's speciality. The spicy, full-bodied wines it produces can smell oddly like peppered gherkins and dill, which may sound offputting, but if yields are low, these wines can age into serious rivals for white Burgundy.

Furmint

This is the most important grape in Hungary's most serious wine, the legendary, long-lived sweet Tokaji. The wine is deep apricot in color and can taste of apricots, too, along with various degrees of what I can only describe as tawny dustiness, according to how traditional the winemaking was.

VINEYARDS IN HUNGARY'S TOKAY OR TOKAJI REGION.

Some common workhorse grapes

Colombard

Known as French Colombard in California, it is quite widely distributed, too. Another grape that makes thin wines high in acidity, Colombard has typically been used for distilling into brandy—or for blending with other more positively flavored or fashionable grapes such as Chardonnay and occasionally Chenin Blanc or Sauvignon Blanc.

Trebbiano/Ugni Blanc

The Italian and French names respectively for a widely planted, high-acid grape that is particularly common in central Italy. Don't expect much flavor.

TREBBIANO GRAPES GROWN IN ITALY'S BAKING
HOT ABRUZZO REGION.

TYPICAL, WELL-TENDED CHAMPAGNE VINEYARD,
WHOSE GRAPES ARE VIRTUALLY ALWAYS BLENDED.

Common white blends

Bordeaux or anywhere
Sauvignon Blanc and Sémillon

Southern France
Some combination of Viognier, Marsanne, Roussanne, Grenache Blanc,
Rolle, Ugni Blanc

Australia
Semillon, Chardonnay

South Africa
Sauvignon Blanc, Chardonnay

Champagne and other top-quality sparkling wine
Chardonnay, Pinot Noir, Pinot Meunier (see page 177)

4. The raw material: red grapes

How to make wine red

The principles of making a white wine were outlined on page 89. If you followed those steps with a black grape you would end up, amazingly enough, with a wine that was white—possibly very pale pink. This is because the flesh of all but a handful of obscure grape varieties is the same color: sludge green. The coloring materials, pigments, are found only in the skin of the grape (which is where the tannins are concentrated, too).

To make a red wine, therefore, or rather to make a wine red, it is essential to keep the grape skins in contact with the must so that the pigments will be attracted out of the skins and into the resultant wine. Conveniently, the heat that is generated by the fermentation process puts everything into a sort of stewing state, and this hastens along the color-extraction process. Otherwise fermentation happens just as with white wines.

On pages 46–47 we examined some of the factors governing how much color a wine has. Some grapes are higher in natural pigments than others, as we shall see. Grenache is a pale grape, as are some clones of Pinot Noir, while Cabernet Sauvignon and Syrah are very thick skinned and therefore great potential donors of coloring matter to the must. Furthermore, the weather in some years encourages thicker skins than others, although nowadays wine producers are so keen on deep-colored reds that they often deliberately try to maximize the amount of color that is extracted in the winery.

By leaving the skins in contact with the must for a protracted period, the winemaker can give extra color to the resultant wine. However, it must not be overdone, as bitter tannic elements will seep out at the same time as the pigments. The must may be left "on the skins," as they say, for anything from a few days to a few weeks. Extra color and tannin can be obtained by pressing the leftover skins and adding that "press wine" to the original wine that was pumped from or run out of the fermentation vat.

Another means of making red wine and extracting a lot of color out of the grapes quickly is carbonic maceration or "whole grape fermentation." Beaujolais is made by a version of this technique, which involves fermenting the grapes without breaking them. The heat builds up inside them and by the action of carbon dioxide in the absence of oxygen, another sort of alcoholic fermentation happens naturally. This makes very supple fruity wines that are not designed for a long life, because they do not contain lots of tannin, but are quite deeply colored. (Incidentally, the grapes at the bottom of the vat are crushed, which means they ferment in the traditional way.)

Skin deep

Take a black grape and peel it. Do the same to a white grape and notice that, without their skins, they are almost indistinguishable. As further evidence of how a white wine can be made from black grapes by carefully running the juice off the skins before fermentation, you need only consider champagne (better still— drink some). The great majority of grapes that go into champagne are dark-skinned—see Chapter 6 for more. Any wine described as a Blanc de Noirs is a white wine made from dark-skinned grapes— quite possible so long as the grapes are pressed very gently and the juice not allowed any contact with the skins.

Quality time

One of the hallmarks of top-quality red Bordeaux, a classed growth wine (one that says *cru classé* on the label and was included in the famous 1855 classification of the Médoc and Graves), is that the wine has been given a fairly long *cuvaison*, time for the must to macerate with the skins. Compare the color of a wine such as this (if you can afford one) with one from the same vintage but from a more ordinary property, a "petit château" that was not included in this classification, or a regular blended Appellation Bordeaux Contrôlée. Notice how the more expensive wine is more deeply flavored, tannic, and long. One of the factors is that it has been left in contact with the skins for longer—as well as having been produced in a better environment or *terroir*.

Carbonic maceration

To examine the fruity charm and deep color given by carbonic maceration and allied techniques, arm yourself with a bottle of Beaujolais. Note the very low-tannin, supple attraction, in which the fruity character is emphasized, which is there to be enjoyed only months after the vintage. See also Gamay on page 148.

Red wine + oak

Oak maturation is much more common for red wines than for whites. Many producers of red wines like to have rows of new small oak casks in their cellars for the extra dimensions of texture and flavor they add to their wines (see pages 98–100). The only deterrent is the cost of the casks themselves, and the work involved in keeping them in good shape.

Wine evaporates fast when it is kept in a porous wooden container, and each cask has to be regularly topped up so that air won't get to work on the wine and spoil it to the point of oxidation. Wood also encourages the natural precipitation of the solid matter left in suspension in the wine after fermentation. This is a good thing— except that the wine will have to be poured, pumped, or "racked," off this deposit to keep it from taking on a stale taste. This means that wine in a well-kept cellar is systematically moved from one cask to another, leaving behind casks that need careful cleaning and reconditioning. Any wine aged in a new wooden (which usually means oak) barrel is likely to cost substantially more than one that has not been treated to this luxurious accommodation.

The alternatives to wooden casks are large vats made of stainless steel and other inert substances, which are free from the dangers of evaporation and much easier to clean. Wines kept in such vats during the settling and "marrying" after fermentation taste simpler and much more obviously fruity than those that take on the layer of oak flavoring offered by wood storage.

Red Bordeaux, as usual, provides an excellent illustration of the effect of oak aging. All classed growth Bordeaux properties (see page 128) will put their wines into small oak casks, the traditional Bordeaux 50 gallon (225-liter) barrique, as will many châteaux, which although not "classified," are making serious wine for a medium to long life. The better regarded the property, the more new casks its owner can afford, and the longer we may have to wait until the wine

SECOND YEAR BARREL CELLAR AT CHÂTEAU MARGAUX IN BORDEAUX.

reaches its peak of maturity. There are some red Bordeaux, generally selling for less than fifteen dollars a bottle, that are specifically designed for a vivacious youth rather than an august old age. They see no wood so that the fresh fruit quality of the wine is emphasized and the liquid is ready to drink only a year or so after the vintage. Compare one of each type to study the effect of Bordeaux's eighteen months or so in small oak casks.

The difference that wood makes

You can use your "standard Cabernet Sauvignon" example (see page 133) to illustrate the combination of oak and red Bordeaux. Choose any youngish wine from the Médoc or Graves, from a specific château. For contrast, choose a straightforward AC red Bordeaux toward the bottom of the price range (one that is too inexpensive to have involved oak aging). Notice that the second wine, which has been kept in an inert material, is light and fruity and the tannin is hardly noticeable. The first wine is much more tannic, and probably has a more complicated flavor. Underneath the cedary oakiness of the first wine is the straightforward fruitiness of the second, but the two wines are as dissimilar as Barolo and Beaujolais. Or, choose any pair of Cabernet Sauvignons from the same region but, by reading the back labels carefully, make sure barrels have been used in the production of one of them.

Types of oak

The number of times an oak cask has been used before affects the final taste of the wine, as outlined already. The newer a cask, the more flavor and tannin it has to give to the wine. The lesser properties of Bordeaux put their wines into casks that have perhaps already been used by a smarter château, and the effects of keeping wines in wood like this are therefore much less obvious than in the finer wines.

The exact method of seasoning and the provenance of the oak can have a bearing on the flavor of any wine kept in cask, as can different intensities of char, and different thicknesses of stave. Oaks divide very generally between American and European—usually French but occasionally eastern European—oaks. French oak tends to taste taut and savory whereas the stereotypical American oak is sweet with more than a whiff of vanilla. Nowadays, however, it is recognized that very well-coopered and seasoned American oak can be every bit as effective as French oak (and better than badly treated French oak)—although it tends to be better suited to quite broad-flavored fruit from a relatively warm climate.

Rioja, Spain's classic red wine, is the most obvious example of a wine that has been matured in American oak (even if more and more Rioja producers are experimenting with French oak). Most red Rioja with a Crianza, Reserva, or Gran Reserva seal on the back of the bottle has spent some time in small American oak casks, usually two years or more, and certainly long enough to give the wine the very distinctive sweet vanilla smell. Red Rioja must be one of the easiest wines to recognize, not because of the grape, for most Riojas are made of a blend of Tempranillo, Garnacha, and possibly other local grape varieties, but because of its American oak flavor, which is its keynote. Another good clue to a Rioja's identity is its relatively light color, made paler by the Riojan practice of moving wine from cask to cask, or "racking," even more often than in most wine regions.

Quality oak

Try to compare a *cru classé* red Bordeaux with a slightly more impoverished château, described as *cru bourgeois* on the label, i.e. one rung down from the 1855 classification. You will note more flavor on the superior wine, with an intense tannic flavor brought about by its newer, more vigorous oak lodgings during infancy.

Rioja and oak

Examine a red Rioja with a seal stating Crianza, Reserva, or Gran Reserva on the back of the bottle. Make sure it has a vintage date of more than three years before, and read the seal on the back of the bottle. In practice, CVNE, Lopez de Heredia, Muga, and La Rioja Alta produce particularly reliable traditionally matured Riojas. Notice the pale red color with a slight tawny tinge. There should never be any sediment in a Rioja, so often has it been racked off its lees. Now take a sniff. There is warmth, sweetness (warm strawberries?), and vanilla there. Take note of how different this opulent vanilla American-oak smell is from the taut cedar French-oak flavor on a fine young red Bordeaux.

Around the world
with Cabernet Sauvignon

Cabernet Sauvignon is the grape variety before which lovers of fine red wine should genuflect.

Pinot Noir may be responsible for a few thousand bottles of great red Burgundy, but Cabernet Sauvignon is the main ingredient in millions of bottles with virtually unparalleled aging potential made all over the world. The reason is its small grapes with thick skins, giving a high ratio of skin to juice, and therefore lots of color and tannin. Furthermore, the Cabernet Sauvignon vine has the winning combination of producing top-quality wine and adapting well to a wide range of climates and soils, while retaining its basic character.

International appeal

It's a bit like the English language. From its original base—in Cabernet Sauvignon's case Bordeaux (which at one time was ruled by the English crown)—it can now be found in a similar form but with different accents worldwide, particularly in America, South Africa, Australia, and New Zealand. With the emphasis on "varietal labeling" in these newer wine regions, it is easy to pick out wines made from this great red grape variety. In Bordeaux, however, Cabernet Sauvignon is hardly ever specified on the label, partly because red Bordeaux (or claret, as it is known in Britain, after the light *clairet* we used to ship from western France in the Middle Ages) is virtually always made from a blend of grapes: typically Cabernet Sauvignon, Merlot, and Cabernet Franc. The other factor is the French appellation contrôlée system's concentration on geography. If you see any of the words listed on page 133 on the label, then the predominant grape is almost certainly Cabernet Sauvignon.

THE OPUS ONE ESTATE IN NAPA VALLEY WHERE CABERNET SAUVIGNON REIGNS SUPREME.

Defining the taste

To form an impression of what Cabernet Sauvignon tastes like when reared in its original Bordelais setting, look for a bottle of red Bordeaux, as fine as you can afford. The standard Bordeaux bottle, with straight sides and a narrow neck, is easy to recognise and it often even has a label proclaiming a château name. The key to likely quality is the

CH CLERC MILON, A "CLASSED GROWTH" PAUILLAC.

"appellation" specified on the label. "Bordeaux" is the most basic appellation and might not present a very distinctive model for your palate picture of Cabernet Sauvignon. "Bordeaux Supérieur" is the same quality level and merely means that the wine is slightly more alcoholic, say 11 percent as opposed to 10.5 percent.

Most really good red Bordeaux carries a more specific appellation. Try to find a wine from some apellation that is respected as a producer of the finest

Cabernet Sauvignon in the world: St Estèphe, Pauillac, St Julien, Margaux, Haut-Médoc, Médoc, Pessac-Léognan, or Graves. This is Cabernet Sauvignon's Bordeaux home on the "left bank" of the Gironde. Any farther from the tempering influence of the sea (such as in St Emilion and Pomerol) and growers can have difficulty ripening Cabernet Sauvignon properly. Specific châteaux whose vineyards are planted with a high proportion of Cabernet Sauvignon, and whose wines are therefore very good examples of the varietal's characteristics, include (you should be so rich) Châteaux Latour, Mouton-Rothschild, d'Issan, du Tertre, Pouget, and La Louvière. The Cabernet grape should, however, dominate in the blend of any wine with the appellations specified above.

Notice in your sample of fine Bordeaux Cabernet the intensity of everything; color, flavor, and length are all very pronounced in this wine. The only ingredient in which red Bordeaux is relatively short is alcohol.

Smell the wine and try to register that black currant flavor. This grape aroma may be overlaid with the flavor of oak, if the wine has been aged in new oak barrels. For an example of the pure grape aroma, stick to the least expensive basic Bordeaux.

**CABERNET SAUVIGNON—BLUE GRAPES,
THICK SKINS, AND HARD (VINE) WOOD.**

The Cabernet grape

Bear in mind that, contrary to popular opinion, Cabernet Sauvignon is not the most planted variety in Bordeaux (see page 140). Most red wines carrying the general appellation Bordeaux will be made in the Cabernet Sauvignon style, however, even though they may contain a high proportion of other Bordeaux grapes.

The Cabernet grape itself is small and very dark blue, grows in tight clusters, and, when pressed and fermented, usually has lots of tannin and color to give to the must. The keynotes of youthful, fully ripe Cabernet are a very deep purple ink color, the aroma of blackcurrants (not totally unlike the related Sauvignon Blanc), and, usually, lots of acidity and tannin. Underripe Cabernet Sauvignon can be too lean and tart and often smells very grassy, leafy, or "herbaceous." Red Bordeaux, unlike some hot-country Cabernets, is only light to medium bodied, but its flavor is very intense and there is often a very lingering finish. A good Cabernet wine is capable of aging superbly and, indeed, many, with their high level of tannin, demand it.

Around the world

To get a suitably well-informed impression of Cabernet Sauvignon, you should probably force yourself to sample the huge range of wines made from the grape around the world. Outside Bordeaux, but still in France, Cabernet Sauvignon is grown in the outlying regions of southwest France, such as Bergerac and Madiran, in the Languedoc, and to a certain extent in Provence (where it is blended with Syrah). It is also grown increasingly in the Loire, where it may struggle to ripen in some years, and is routinely blended with the other Cabernet, Cabernet Franc (see page 138). Try to taste as much Cabernet Sauvignon as possible. Examples from eastern Europe such as Bulgarian, Romanian, and Hungarian tend to be very straightforward and good value—but watch out for heavy-handed oaking on the Bulgarians. Chile is a great source of more aromatic Cabernet Sauvignon, without an excess of alcohol (often not that much tannin) and an unmistakable floral perfume. Argentine Cabernets are slightly more concentrated and in some cases so thick they are almost syrupy. Try to extract the Cabernet character from each of these wines whenever you have the chance to taste them.

Cabernet and climate

Because Cabernet Sauvignon is grown in so many different settings it is particularly useful as an illustration of the effect of local climate on the style of wines produced. Cabernet Sauvignon will never be grown in quite as wide a range of places as Chardonnay because it is a much later-ripening vine and can only be grown successfully in reasonably warm climates.

Bordeaux, with its temperate climate on the Atlantic seaboard, can have difficulty getting its Cabernets fully ripe in some years, but because it is at this limit of ripening, the best wines display the quintessence of the variety. They have lots of very subtle fruit but are not too high in alcohol and tend to have appetizing levels of both tannin and acidity. These are moderate wines that are ultra-digestible. Cabernet Sauvignons produced in New Zealand, however, in a generally cooler climate, tend to be even lighter in body and noticeably more tart. Washington State Cabernets and some of those produced in the cooler parts of northeast Italy

YOUNG VINES TRAINED UP POSTS IN CLARE VALLEY,
ONE OF SOUTH AUSTRALIA'S COOLER WINE AREAS.

represent the slightly fuller, fruitier style of Cabernet that results from, among other things, rather hotter summers than are usual in Bordeaux and New Zealand.

To see the most dramatic examples of the impact of unmitigated sunshine on a red grape variety in general, and on Cabernet Sauvignon in particular, look at one of California's heavy-weights. Full-bodied, ripe-to-the-point-of-plumminess Cabernets are not difficult to find here; indeed, it takes a degree of winemaking skill to produce a California Cabernet that is not too high in alcohol and everything else, too. Look at the depth of color in these wines. When you look down into it, you will find it difficult to locate the bottom of the glass through the wine. The smell will be so strong, it will have blackcurrant and practically every other fruit you can imagine. Many sought-after Napa Cabernets even have a hint of mint or eucalyptus overlaid. In fact, a certain mintiness is a good giveaway to a California Cabernet—although some of the best can also betray a certain dusty or mineral quality that is found in some top-quality red Bordeaux.

Other examples of hot-country Cabernets, with predictable effects on color and alcohol levels, are the Lebanese Château Musar (though Cabernet is here blended with Rhône grapes) and many Australian Cabernets. A common sight in wines from these two countries, both of whose reds often taste very hot, is a blackish tinge. Australian Cabernets tend to be very minty and "thick," with a certain amount of both sweetness and acidity. Coonawarra is one of Australia's most established areas for Cabernet.

South African Cabernets tend to be more marked by blackcurrant notes and some of them have quite high acidity—not because the climate is particularly cool, but because many of the vines suffer from a virus that prevents the grapes from ripening fully. Meerlust's Rubicon bottling is one of the most respected South African Cabernet Sauvignons.

Cool Bordeaux

Your first example of red Bordeaux, from page 133, will do admirably to demonstrate Cabernet Sauvignon from a temperate climate. Notice that you find it rather appetizing. Another glass with food would be pretty nice, though the high level of tannin in youthful red Bordeaux means that it is difficult to drink without food, and seems even tougher if served too cool. Red Bordeaux has been described as the ultimate beverage wine. Inexpensive Italian or New Zealand Cabernets are often so light and dry they can be almost weedy, and you may have to hunt for the flavor.

California Cabernet

Most decent California Cabernets will prove the point about the difference a hottish climate makes to the richness of the wine made there. Choose your example by the alcohol content on the label. Cabernets of 14 percent are by no

means uncommon in California. You will notice, as well as the viscosity and the burn in the finish of such a high-alcohol wine, much less acidity than in your Bordeaux example and a richness that tastes almost sweet. Watch out for the distinctive minty, eucalyptus flavor in some more expensive California Cabernets, made famous by Heitz Martha's Vineyard. Some California Cabernets can, however, be confused with some red Bordeaux. A youthful, very concentrated red Bordeaux from a ripe year that is high in extract because it has had a long *cuvaison* can seem very like the deep-colored, intense wines of California—especially since top producers in California use exactly the same sort of barrels as the Bordelais (sometimes even from the same cooper). Look for a wine with the lower alcohol level as this is a good indication that the wine was made on the French side of the Atlantic.

The other Cabernet

Although "blending" is seen as a dirty word by so many wine drinkers, the most famous wine in the world, red Bordeaux, is very much a blended wine. Bordeaux wine farms, usually called Château Quelquechose, are invariably planted with a mixture of grapes. Even those such as the top Médoc and Graves wines, which are predominantly Cabernet Sauvignon, will usually have a bit of Cabernet Franc or Merlot planted alongside and blended into the final wine. This partly reflects prudent farming: Merlot flowers and ripens earlier than the Cabernets so if, in this variable climate, the weather is poor during the flowering of one variety, the other variety will compensate.

The most common "other grape" is Cabernet Franc. It has often been rather contemptuously dismissed as a lesser (less tannic, less concentrated) version of the Cabernet Sauvignon, but its stock has risen after the discovery that in fact, it, with Sauvignon Blanc, is the parent of the more famous and better-traveled Cabernet Sauvignon. And, after all, Château Cheval Blanc, the great first growth of St. Emilion, is made up of two-thirds Cabernet Franc. Cabernet Franc is much more widely planted than Cabernet Sauvignon in St. Emilion, nearby Pomerol, and the rest of the "right bank" of the Gironde because the climate there is generally too cool to ripen the later Cabernet Sauvignon reliably.

Cabernet Franc tastes similar to Cabernet Sauvignon, but is usually even more herbaceous and lighter bodied. And because the grapes themselves are bigger, the wines are less tannic and are lighter colored. For these reasons, Cabernet Franc–based wines tend to be more accessible and mature earlier than Cabernet Sauvignons. The Cabernet Franc grape is planted extensively in the middle Loire Valley, and in northern Italy, where it produces luscious, fruity wines with an edge of acidity and grassiness. For blending purposes, Cabernet Franc is increasingly planted anywhere Cabernet Sauvignon is grown, but varietal Cabernet Franc wines are increasingly common—especially in slightly cooler wine regions such as Washington State and New Zealand.

If you see the word Cabernet on an Italian wine label, then it is almost certainly predominantly Cabernet Franc, planted much more widely there than Cabernet Sauvignon. Friuli and Trentino, up in the far northeast, turn out some very good-value wines of this type, and others distinctly light on character.

CHINON—ONE OF CABERNET FRANC'S
MOST DELICIOUS FORMS.

There are many similarities between them, but you should be able to distinguish a Cabernet Franc from a Cabernet Sauvignon by its lower tannin content, color, and body. When Cabernet Sauvignon is cultivated in a very cool climate, however, it can taste remarkably like Cabernet Franc (as in some New Zealand reds, for example).

Cabernet Franc— defining the taste

For pure, unblended Cabernet Franc, try to taste a red Loire such as Chinon, Bourgueil, or slightly more intense and long lived, St. Nicolas de Bourgueil. There is a certain juiciness, though it is less fruity than Beaujolais. My trigger term is "pencil shavings" for the distinctive aroma of these wines— and I mean the wood part rather than the lead.

Try to taste one of the Loire or Italian Cabernets alongside a Cabernet Sauvignon, preferably a red Bordeaux from the Médoc, of the same age. Taste the Cabernet Sauvignon second because its much higher tannin content will pucker up your mouth, leaving a coating of astringency all over it. Notice also how much more body and color the red Bordeaux has compared to the other—and surely it seems drier?

Merlot, the fruitcake variety

Merlot is to St. Emilion and Pomerol what Cabernet Sauvignon is to Médoc and Graves.

The variety that predominates on this "right bank" is a wonderfully attractive supple sort of grape that, when properly vinified, turns out rich, spicy wines with all the plummy sort of appeal of a rich fruitcake. So appealing can it be, in fact, that some top Pomerols such as Château Pétrus and Le Pin, both made almost entirely of Merlot, can lay claim to be the world's most expensive wines.

Merlot, which reaches its apogee in St. Emilion and Pomerol, ripens easily and produces wines that taste quite sweet. This counterbalances what tannin there may be to make them seem much softer than an equivalent Cabernet Sauvignon. A good Merlot-based wine often has a sort of rich velvety texture with a heady, complex aroma that some tasters have variously described as gunshot, pheasant, and gamey. I'm spirited more to the spice shelf than the game parlor myself.

In slightly less distinguished form, Merlot is the most planted grape variety throughout Bordeaux. This means that Merlot is almost certainly the dominant variety in any wine labeled appellation Bordeaux contrôlée. Such wines tend to be produced at fairly high yields and in a temperate rather than warm climate, so most of them are fairly light in color, body, and flavor. They are made to the model of long-lasting Médoc, however (which may or may not be a good thing), so they tend to have some tannins, highish acidity, and a dry finish.

MERLOT GRAPES IN
ST. EMILION,
BORDEAUX. THEY
USUALLY HAVE
THINNER SKINS
THAN CABERNET.

Defining the taste

It should not be too difficult to find a good, toothsome example of a Merlot-based red Bordeaux. Any St. Emilion would do, as indeed would any wine that has St. Emilion on the label in any form (there are all sorts of complicated and tiny appellations such as Montagne-St. Emilion, St. Georges-St. Emilion, and various other hyphenated communes). A Pomerol would be an even better example, as it is likely to contain a higher proportion of Merlot. Notice the greater viscosity and slightly higher alcohol content in a Merlot than in a Cabernet Sauvignon. There is also a warm, sun-baked sort of flavor that is reminiscent of very ripe fruit, almost a plummy fruitcake. The level of tannin seems less marked than in Cabernet Sauvignon, and there is much more richness than in Cabernet Franc.

Merlot in the US

In the US, Merlot, celebrated for its relatively low tannins and acid and superficial sweetness, was well-placed to benefit from the huge consumer swing from white wine to red in the 1990s. It has in effect become "red Chardonnay," so popular is it—although many California examples (and there are many California examples) are extremely light on varietal character to say the least. Distinctly superior, and extremely hedonistic, examples are made by the likes of Duckhorn, Harrison, Havens, Matanzas Creek, Shafer, St. Francis, and Silverado.

Farther north, Washington State is one of the very few New World wine regions that have established a reputation specifically for Merlot, and is turning out very attractive, supple examples, although the lack of winter-hardiness of the vine (compared to the Cabernets) has proved a problem in some years. Andrew Will has made particularly fine Merlots.

One extremely good-value source of Merlot is Chile, where the vine seems to have adapted itself particularly well and even inexpensive examples can demonstrate much of the velvety texture of a good Merlot. Casa Lapostolle makes particularly voluptuous examples. Elsewhere in the New World, Merlot is growing in popularity and plantings are increasingly rapidly in Australia, New Zealand, and South Africa.

MERLOT HAS ALSO TRAVELED AS FAR AS NEW ZEALAND.

Merlot, like Cabernet Franc, has long been planted in the north of Italy, with very variable results—although there are some seriously ambitious examples such as Castello di Ama's in Tuscany. Another source of generally undistinguished Merlot is the Languedoc in southern France. Such wines tend to be vaguely sweet and red with, occasionally, a grassy aroma.

Only the best

Compare your St. Emilion or Pomerol standard Merlot example with an inexpensive Merlot from Italy, the Languedoc (a Vin de Pays d'Oc), or California. You can tell just from the color that the cheaper specimen is much thinner and paler. It will taste that way, too, with pronounced acidity spun out over a rather watery taste. A pale (red) color, often rather dull, is an indication that the vine yield was too high for quality.

Comparison of St. Emilion/Pomerol with such a wine illustrates well the result of asking too much of a vine in terms of grape production. There are stringent controls on most French appellations as to exactly how much wine each hectare of vines may produce. A good property may well do an additional summer prune to further restrict yield to make only, say, 3000 quarts of wine for every 2.5 acres. A basic Merlot from California's Central Valley, France's Languedoc, or Italy's Veneto may have been made to about three or four times this yield, and the taste is obviously "stretched" accordingly. The result is a much thinner, less exciting wine, although there are also variables other than yield of course—climate and clone being the two obvious ones.

The fabulously
fussy Pinot Noir

Just as Cabernet Sauvignon is responsible for most of the great red wines of Bordeaux, Pinot Noir is solely responsible for all the great red Burgundies.

No red grape other than Pinot is allowed into such appellations as Gevrey-Chambertin, Chambolle-Musigny, Clos de Vougeot, Nuits-St.-Georges, Aloxe-Corton, Beaune, Pommard, and Volnay. When grown in the finest vineyards of the famous Côte d'Or, the "golden slope" of Burgundy, in a good year and vinified by a careful winemaker, it can produce fabulous wine. "Ethereal," "soft and velvety," "iron hand in a velvet glove," "rich and scented" are all descriptions of great red Burgundy.

If red Bordeaux is a reasonably reliable commodity, red Burgundy can be infuriatingly variable. The least gifted or most cynical winemakers turn out overpriced disappointments. But when Burgundy is good—as it is increasingly, now that a decent winemaking education and some overseas travel has become the norm for the current generation of winemakers in Burgundy—it is more thrilling than all but a handful of red wines from Bordeaux.

Good Pinot is so inspiring that wine producers all over the world have been tempted to try their hand with the grape, so it is worth training your palate to recognize it. A good Pinot is slightly sweet and definitely more gently perfumed than the rather uncompromising Cabernet. Tannin is much less marked, for Pinot is considerably less "pippy" and the skins are much thinner. This also accounts for the Pinot's relatively light color (although very serious wine estates, called *domaines* in Burgundy, such as the low-yielding Domaine de la Romanée Conti, ferment the wine on the skins for so long that they manage to extract quite a good depth of color). Most Pinots have less body than the average Cabernet and their appeal is perhaps more subtle. It is easy to see why red Bordeaux was described as masculine and Burgundy as feminine, however much one resists such facile descriptions. Some tasters describe the scent of Pinot as boiled beetroot, others as dead game. In young Pinot there is the very definite smell of raspberries, while in middle age it takes on definite vegetal overtones.

Defining the taste

For the taste of true Pinot fruit you would be well advised to go for one of the lesser appellations of Burgundy. Not only do they cost a fraction of the big names, they are also usually more reliable (at their quality level). These are not wines for keeping, but the well-made ones offer good simple Pinot flavor. Plain old appellation Bourgogne (French for Burgundy) from a reliable individual grower (*domaine*) such as Robert Chevillon or Tollot-Beaut is a good one to head for. Notice that the wines are fairly pale and light and have a fruity nose—reminding me of raspberries, while others think of strawberries or violets. There is something soft and sweet about the wine, and little tannin (though there may be quite a lot of acidity in a not-so-good vintage, because the region is so far from the Equator). Probably the cheapest way of tasting Pinot Noir is via a bottle of sweetish red so labeled from California or Chile (Cono Sur is a reliable producer). The flavor won't be the purest. It may even be rather jammy. But it's a start.

Regional differences

The Côte d'Or, Burgundy's heartland, is made up of the northern part, the Côte de Nuits centred on Nuits-St.-Georges, and the southern Côte de Beaune, dominated by the town of Beaune. Traditionally, the wines of the Côte de Nuits are firmer and longer lasting than the softer, lighter style of the Côte de Beaune. In practice, the name of the producer is a much better guide to likely style and quality than even the name of the appellation. All of these wines are expensive, but if you have lots of money and patience you can build up your own impressions of the different producers. The briefest of brief outlines of mine are shown in the table opposite.

THE PINE CONE-LIKE BUNCHES OF PINOT NOIR.

Cheaper than those from the Côte d'Or, and usually rather lighter and tarter, are the wines from its upper hinterland, Hautes Côtes de Nuits and Beaune. Other examples of affordable red Burgundy made from the Pinot grape come from the Côte Chalonnaise to the south. Rully, Givry, and Mercurey are the names to look for here. Any farther south and you are into Gamay country (see page 148).

Producers of Pinot Noir

Côte d'Or Burgundy

The most exciting provenance of Côte d'Or Burgundy is the individual *domaine*, provided it is one of the increasing number that is quality conscious. A significant proportion of Burgundy's output is, however, bottled by the much bigger merchants or "négociants" and they have very varying reputations. Here are some of the more reliable for red wine:

Bouchard Père et Fils—good vineyards around Beaune, being revitalized.
Joseph Drouhin—extremely rigorous, the best of the new methods grafted onto traditional techniques. Relatively light, pure wines.
Louis Jadot—rich and firm.

Côte Chalonnaise

These wines are like country cousins of those from the Côte d'Or to the north. Quality is generally much more dependable than on the Côte d'Or, even if it does not hit such heights, so most bottles of Rully, Givry, and Mercurey will serve as your example for comparison with a bottle from the Burgundian heartland to the north. Notice that these Côte Chalonnaise wines are earthier, lighter, and leaner than fine Côte d'Or wines.

Alsace, Sancerre, and Champagne

Alsace Pinot struggles to impress, for it is usually just a bit too light, and sometimes sweet like German Pinot Noir, or Spätburgunder. Sancerre Rouge and Rosé are made from Pinot and most examples demonstrate a bit of Pinot scent and a light color. They may be chaptalized fairly heavily to bring them up to an acceptable alcoholic strength. If you ever find a champagne that is described as a Blanc de Noirs (Bollinger occasionally make one from their intense and ancient Vieilles Vignes of Pinot) it will be pure Pinot, as is the irresistibly named Bouzy Rouge.

PINOT NOIR VINE IN VOSNE-ROMANÉE, BURGUNDY. YOU CAN
TELL IT IS OLD BY THE THICKNESS OF THE TRUNK.

Vintage and climate

Vintages for red Burgundy can vary considerably—and generally
more than for white Burgundy since Chardonnay is a much less
fussy vine than the delicate Pinot Noir. Pinots in general are ready
to drink long before Cabernets, owing to their lower tannin content
and lighter weight.

Some Pinot Noir is grown in other parts of northeastern
France: in Alsace (where it produces a dark rosé, illustrating well

how difficult it is to get a deep-colored Pinot even in a region whose white wines regularly notch up an alcohol content of 13 percent); in the Jura and Sancerre, where it is responsible for pale reds and even paler rosés; and in Champagne, where it is blended with Chardonnay and a related, slightly coarser grape called Pinot Meunier to produce the world's most famous sparkling wine. Pure Pinot is available as a still wine of Champagne sold as Coteaux Champenois Rouge, and villages such as Bouzy and Cumières are famous for it.

Pinot is a grape that ripens relatively early, so to make interesting wine it has to be grown somewhere relatively cool, so that the growing season is long enough to develop sufficient flavor elements. In California, for example, fine Pinot Noir is produced only in areas substantially cooled by Pacific fogs, such as the Russian River valley of Sonoma, the vineyards of the Central Coast around Santa Barbara, and in isolated high altitude vineyards such as those of Chalone and Calera. These wines tend to have a direct fruitiness often lacking in young red Burgundy.

Wine producers in the cooler climes of Oregon to the north have set their caps at rivaling Burgundy eventually, although autumn rains are a constant threat and there is considerable vintage variation. Some of the most successful producers of the States' particularly juicy style of Pinot are Archery Summit, Beaux Frères, Brick House, Cristom, Domaine Drouhin, Ponzi, WillaKenzie, and Ken Wright.

Parts of New Zealand, which is another relatively cool vine-growing environment, show promise for Pinot Noir. Much of Australia is too hot for fine Pinot Noir, but Tasmania and parts of the state of Victoria, notably but not exclusively Yarra Valley, clearly have real potential.

Pinot Noir is also grown all over eastern and southeastern Europe under a variety of aliases: Pinot Nero in northern Italy, Blauburgunder in Austria, Spätburgunder in Germany, and Blauer Burgunder in the eastern, German-speaking parts of Switzerland, where it is increasingly planted and highly regarded.

There have been a few successful Pinot Noirs in the cooler vineyards of Chile and South Africa. Much more common in South Africa is a beefy red grape called Pinotage, which is a cross between Pinot Noir and Cinsaut, the rough and vigorous southern Rhône grape that was once called Hermitage (see page 164).

Gamay the gulpable

Gamay, the grape responsible for Beaujolais, is particularly easy to recognize. Even the color is distinctive: lightish crimson with a purplish tinge, making Beaujolais one of the "bluest" wines in the world.

The smell is even more tell-tale, and even more difficult to describe than that of other grapes. Gamay is always high in refreshing acidity (most of these wines are really "white" in function if not in hue) and just one sniff will have your tongue crinkling in anticipation. Gamay usually produces fairly lightweight wines, but you may come across examples that seem medium or even full bodied.

A high proportion of all Gamay grapes are turned into wine using the carbonic maceration method referred to on pages 127–128. This technique confers its own aromas on a wine, somewhere between banana (or rather what flavor technologists consider is banana flavor) and nail polish. The standard tasting note on Beaujolais is always "fresh and fruity," the freshness being that acidity, and the fruitiness the very simple but undeniable appeal of the Gamay grape. You know when you smell it that it is not a great wine, but it is so eminently gulpable that any genuine well-made example will woo you into the glass.

Youthful Gamay

Gamay-based wines are very rarely suitable for aging. Their chief purpose is to refresh and give gulping pleasure while youthful—still in the nursery in the case of Beaujolais Nouveau. This Beaujolais is fermented, stabilized, and bottled super-fast—by November 15 after the vintage.

A *cru* Beaujolais, from one of the ten special villages, can gain depth and interest for about five years after the good vintage, and the wines from the Moulin-à-Vent *cru* can age into an almost Burgundian state of maturity. Look for the following names on the label to enjoy superior Beaujolais from these *crus*: Fleurie, Chiroubles, St. Amour, Chénas, Juliénas, Brouilly, Côte de Brouilly, Morgon, Moulin-à-Vent. A wine labeled Beaujolais-Villages will usually taste a little firmer and juicer than a straight Beaujolais, while these *cru* wines have positive character of their own.

The grape that makes such luscious wines in the Beaujolais region nevertheless turns out some very ordinary stuff under

**THE ROLLING HILLS OF
BEAUJOLAIS, SOME OF
THE MOST EVOCATIVE
FRENCH COUNTRYSIDE.**

theory

the name of Mâcon Rouge, geographically between the Côte
Chalonnaise and Beaujolais.

Other Gamay-based French wines are usually called Gamay
on the label (Beaujolais very rarely is) and are made in Touraine
on the Loire, in the Ardèche and the Côtes d'Auvergne, du Forez
and Roannaises.

Gamay is currently rather unfashionable and not that much
planted outside France as consumers have been taught to associate
deep colors and concentrated flavors with quality in a red wine. This
is a shame.

A refreshing taste

To form your impression of Gamay
look for Beaujolais that has been
bottled in the region, preferably at
the *domaine* where the grapes
were grown. One example from
Duboeuf should be enough to
imprint that Gamay character on
your memory. Remember that a
light-bodied red wine, such as the
sort of Beaujolais the Gamay
produces, can take a certain
amount of chilling if you want a
drink for refreshment. In any case
the Gamay is not a grape that gives
off so many fascinating nuances of
flavor that you need to encourage
this vaporization by warmth.
Standard practice in the region
itself is to serve Beaujolais "cellar
cool," at about 52ºF (11ºC).
Beaujolais is the perfect wine for
circumstances in which you can't
govern serving temperature too
strictly, such as on a picnic. It can
bear a wide range of temperatures,
so if you chill it before setting off
you will probably still enjoy it at the
much warmer temperature it
reaches by the end of your picnic.

practice

GAMAY THE GULPABLE   **149**

theory

Syrah, black as night

*Until a few years ago, the Syrah grape was largely confined to
Australia, where it is known as Shiraz, and two small strips of
steep vineyard on the banks of the northern Rhône just south of Lyons,
where it produces wines called Côte Rôtie, Hermitage,
Crozes Hermitage, St. Joseph, and Cornas.*

In the first edition of this book in 1983 I wrote: "it is strange that the
Syrah grape is not cultivated more widely when it is capable of
producing such thrilling, long-lived wines." This observation must
have taken root because today there is widespread experimentation
with Syrah (sometimes called Shiraz) in places as diverse as Toledo
in Spain, Alentejo in Portugal, Puglia and Tuscany in Italy,
Aconcagua in Chile, Washington State and the Central Coast,
California in the US, and Stellenbosch in South Africa—and the
grape is now also planted all over southern France.

**SYRAH IN ITS HOMELAND,
THE NORTHERN RHÔNE.**

The resultant wine varies according to how ripe the grapes get. Syrah in the northern Rhône, where the grapes rarely suffer an excess of heat, is a very dark, almost black color, extremely dry and tannic with a distinctive "essence-of-something" flavor that I variously call black pepper or even, in less-than-perfectly-ripe examples, burnt rubber.

Early examples from warm regions new to growing Syrah were often much more exotic, almost soft, with lots of ripe, broad fruit and a certain savory quality at the end of the palate.

Australian Shiraz is different again. Only in the coolest spots of Victoria or Coonawarra in cooler vintages does it exhibit much of the black pepper character; in general it is extremely rich, full bodied, viscous, often fairly tannic (sometimes from added tannin) but almost sweet and chocolaty—especially from relatively hot spots such as the Barossa Valley.

Defining the taste

A first-class and not-too-expensive way to acquaint yourself with the taste of well-made French Syrah would be to find a bottle of Crozes Hermitage from a producer as reliable as Alain Graillot, Albert Belle, or Paul Jaboulet Aîné. Notice how intense the color and flavor are. The tannin is marked but combined with a flavor quite unlike Cabernet Sauvignon—there is nothing in this wine that would remind you of blackcurrants. The nearest fruit taste would be mulberries perhaps, but the Syrah is surely more mineral than vegetable (only Pinot and Mourvèdre are animal!) and extremely dry at the end. You could probably find a Syrah de l'Ardèche even more cheaply. Look for hints of black pepper and burnt rubber.

Compare your North Rhône Syrah with a bottle of Australian Shiraz. Penfolds are past masters of the concentrated South Australian style, but such wines are not difficult to find from the likes of Hardy's, d'Arenberg, Peter Lehmann, and a host of others. Try to find a Shiraz with a more specific geographical unit on the label than "South-Eastern Australia" which is an umbrella appellation that allows bottlers to blend in some cheaper fruit from the irrigated interior. Barossa or McLaren Vale would be perfect. Notice how much "thicker" and sweeter the Australian wine is.

SYRAH BECOMES SHIRAZ IN SOUTH AUSTRALIA'S BAROSSA VALLEY.

Now an international traveler

Syrah has long been grown to a limited extent in the southern part of the Rhône Valley, too, and is increasingly cultivated by quality-conscious producers throughout the Languedoc's vast acreage of vineyards in southern France. It is very much a noble grape, designed for a long life and able to add firmness and an intriguing spiciness to blends of other grape varieties (typically Grenache, Mourvèdre, Cinsault, and Carignan) in Châteauneuf-du-Pape, Gigondas, or Côtes-du-Rhône in the southern Rhône Valley, or such Languedoc appellations as Costières de Nîmes, Coteaux du Languedoc, Faugères, St. Chinian, Minervois, and Corbières.

In California, plantings of Syrah have been increasing rapidly, spurred on by the self-styled "Rhône Rangers," who led a campaign for more diversity in the state's vineyards. Joseph Phelps, Bonny Doon, Alban, Cline, and Jade Mountain are all very competent practitioners—and the wines tend more to the French model than the Australian, but with an extra layer of ripeness.

Southern France

Try to find a southern French wine labeled Syrah, or one that your retailer can tell you has a dominant proportion of Syrah grapes in the blend. There are hundreds of such bottlings from interesting individual *domaines* throughout the Languedoc. Notice how this wine seems to split the difference between the North Rhône and South Australian versions. In good examples of this wine there is a definite savory, almost salty, character, and a real gloss to the texture.

Try to get your hands on a Syrah or Shiraz from somewhere other than France or Australia. Compare your impressions with those of your French Syrah and Australian Shiraz. Notice the opulence and sweetness of the wine compared with the French example, and how it is almost certainly less tannic than the Australian.

theory

practice

GRENACHE IS FAMOUS
FOR MANAGING TO GROW
BUSHLIKE IN
CHÂTEAUNEUF-DU-PAPE'S
STONY VINEYARDS.

Grenache and other Rhône grapes

While some of the beefier Châteauneuf-du-Papes and other southern Rhône wines may well contain a bit of Syrah, Grenache Noir is the most commonly planted grape there.

Grenache Noir is distinguished by an unusual combination of paleness of color and high alcohol, and has a sweet, fruity flavor that is a bit like a very strong mixture of Beaujolais and a good Pinot Noir—plus herbiness. Widely grown in Provence, it seems to pick up a little of that region's scent of lavender and wild thyme.

Most Châteauneuf and other southern Rhône wines are made from a mixture of grapes and it can be interesting to taste them knowing this. See if you can notice that they, like another blend, Rioja, taste more soupy—more like a mixture of different flavors than one dominant one. The great Château Rayas, however, that specialize in making a wine from Grenache only. This provides a good opportunity to come to grips with the flavor of this grape, which—as Garnacha—is an ingredient with Tempranillo in the typical red Rioja blend. It is particularly important in Priorat and Navarra.

Because of its light color and fruitiness, Grenache is in great demand as chief ingredient for pink wine and predominates in the taste of the powerful rosés of Tavel and Lirac, and in many of the "tourist rosés" of Provence. Notice the high alcohol content, pale color, and a certain lusciousness, even if the wine is basically dry. Most rosés are made in the same way as red wines, except that the must is run off the skins after a much shorter time so that much less coloring matter is absorbed. This is how wines described as "blush" wines are made, and a prime example is White Zinfandel, a wine made from dark-skinned grapes that is pale pink because it is left in contact with those skins for such a short time.

Defining the taste

Each time you taste a Châteauneuf-du-Pape, try to assess how much Syrah it contains. If you don't taste much Syrah, then the predominant grape variety is probably Grenache. The average Châteauneuf contains about 10 percent Syrah, 65 percent Grenache and a mixture of other local grape varieties, though some Châteauneufs are made without any Syrah at all. Notice just how sweet, ripe, spicy, and alcoholic Grenache is.

Grenache and rosé

Any Tavel or Lirac and most Provence rosés will demonstrate the Grenache as a rosé. Notice that it can be as full bodied as a red wine, and have just as much acidity as a white. See if you can smell Provençal herbs in these wines. Basic pink wines from Provence may have little flavor though.

Some other southern French red grapes

Mourvèdre, as it is known in France, is a grape that is commonly blended with Syrah and Grenache.

In Spain its most common name is Monastrell, and at various times and places (notably by immigrant grape growers in California and Australia earlier this century) it has been called Mataro. Its French stronghold is Bandol, where it is the main grape in this gamey, herby wine. Mourvèdre needs warmth to ripen fully, so it is not planted much north of Châteauneuf-du-Pape. Used for blending in the Languedoc appellations mentioned on page 152, it can add an opulent note to Syrah, Grenache, and Carignan.

The vine covers far more acreage in Spain, however, where as Monastrell it is planted all along the southern Mediterranean coast. It is not particularly highly regarded in Spain as it tends to reach almost rudely high alcohol levels and can easily lack acid (though not color). There have been some quite successful experiments blending it with the more structured Merlot.

In California and Australia, Mataro has long since been renamed Mourvèdre and is usually blended with Syrah and/or Grenache. It is possible to find varietal Mourvèdre, however, from the likes of Jade Mountain and Cline Cellars in California.

Carignan was for years by far the most planted grape in France because it was so common on the high-yielding plains of the Languedoc. It was extremely easy to grow in an era when growers did not bother using wires to expose fruit and leaves to sunshine and simply grew vines in untidy bushes that sprawled over the vineyard. The resulting wine was often extremely tough (though carbonic maceration was often used to try to counteract this) and had a rank, coarse flavor.

practice

Mourvèdre

To form your palate picture of Mourvèdre, locate a Bandol, Spanish Monastrell, or varietal Mourvèdre. Notice how animal the flavor can be. In less ripe versions it tends to be spicy; in very ripe versions its flavor can be somewhere between raw meat and wet fur. Personally, I prefer it in a blend.

Carignan

Any very basic French red table wine (labeled Vin de Table) is likely to contain a high proportion of Carignan. Notice that nasty flavor and rigidity at the back of the palate.

Much of this unappetizing Carignan has been pulled out, however, and throughout the hills of the Languedoc appellations there are examples of old, low-yielding Carignan vines that can produce much more sumptuous wine. Good examples are made by Domaine d'Aupilhac in Coteaux du Languedoc and Château de Lastours in Corbières. This grape is called Carignane in California, where there are some even older vines producing wine good enough to be included in the odd red blend from Ridge Vineyards. It is not a noble grape, however.

Nebbiolo, Piedmont's greatest

Italophiles wake up. Your time has come at last. The great wines of Italy have not been mentioned so far because they are typically made from (red) grapes that are not often encountered outside Italy.

For years Italy was an island in terms of wine production and appreciation, but the "classic" grapes of the rest of Europe have been gaining ground—quite literally—all over the country and especially in the northeast. These "new" Cabernets, Pinots, Rieslings, and Chardonnays apart, most of the grapes grown in Italy are foreign in both name and taste to most non-Italians.

Italy's greatest wines come from pockets of cooler vineyards, usually by virtue of altitude, and its most famous fine wine region is Piedmont. Here the Nebbiolo grape is king, and the locals claim for their most famous wine (as others have done elsewhere) that Barolo is the "king of wines and wine of kings." Nebbiolo gets its name from the mist or *nebbia* that can shroud the vineyards of these Alpine foothills in the autumn, and is grown throughout the region to produce its longest-living wines.

The thick-skinned Nebbiolo is a very tannic grape that translates into very tannic, dark-colored wines—though new winemaking techniques in the vineyard and cellar have tended to make more approachable wines since the mid-1970s. The hallmark of Nebbiolo is its bouquet, one of those smells that have non-wine-drinkers screeching with incredulous mirth when they read the classic descriptions: roses, violets, tar, truffles, and licorice are all common terms of appreciation for this very dry, full-bodied tannic wine. In structure a good young Nebbiolo can be quite like a good young Syrah, but there is usually more obvious fruit and scent in a fine Nebbiolo than in most youthful Syrah-based wines. Nebbiolo often turns orange sooner, and I sometimes find the great Italian Piedmont grape tastes rather pruney.

The trouble with wines made from Nebbiolo is that, although they all come from this corner of northwest Italy, there can be enormous variation in quality and style. Barolo and its slightly lighter neighbor Barbaresco are the most famous, but Boca, Carema, Fara, Gattinara, Ghemme, Lessona, Sizzano, Spanna, and wines labeled as Nebbiolo are all based on the grape. Barolo is fashioned to last the longest, but a good Barbaresco can be less of an

theory

assault on the senses. Most of these wines are very strong; Barolo must reach a natural strength of 13 percent at least.

Traditionally, winemakers in Barolo and Barbaresco would ferment the grapes on the stalks as well as with the skins for a protracted period, and then keep them for years in large and ancient chestnut casks—sometimes until the sales order was received, so that a wine might spend twelve years in wood and no time in the bottle before being sold. This tended to make a wine that was naturally very tannic, even drier and leaner of fruit flavor. Only in exceptionally fruity years could the wine be drunk rather than chewed. Things have changed, however. Many winemakers have bought new casks and stainless-steel vats in which to ferment and extract maximum fruit from the grapes (without the tough stalks). The wines are now kept in cask for a much shorter period, and producers purposely allow extended bottle age to soften them, before putting them on the market. You can taste an enormous variation in different styles of these wines.

SERRALUNGA D'ALBA IN BAROLO,
THE HEART OF NEBBIOLO COUNTRY.

Defining the taste

Names to look for among producers of Barolo and Barbaresco include Ceretto, Aldo Conterno, Gaja, Bruno Giacosa, Alfredo Prunotto, Luciano Sandrone, Scavino, Roberto Voerzio. Notice how strong, dry, and tannic the wines are, but try to get to grips with their amazingly intense scent. You may be able to find violets, tar, roses, or even the local white truffles of Alba there—if you've been lucky enough to taste these rarities. With age, these wines, which often have a black hue to them, tend to turn orange faster than the average French wine—particularly if large old vats were used rather than small barrels.

New production methods and taste

Producers who have made modifications to the traditional way of making Barolo and Barbaresco include Ceretto (whose wines are often marketed under the individual vineyard name — surprisingly rare in Italy—such as Bricco Rocche and Bricco Asili), Gaja (whose wines can be very juicy indeed), Alfredo Prunotto, and Luciano Sandrone. Try to compare one of their recent vintages with a more traditionally made wine such as Aldo Conterno's. Notice how much more obvious the fruit is in the "new" wines, and how much more noticeable the tannin is in the "old" ones.

Just as the greatness of great red Burgundy has inspired wine producers the world over to try their hand at Pinot Noir, the quality of Piedmont's top reds has fueled experiments with Nebbiolo from Washington State in the United States to the state of Victoria in Australia. So far, those haunting perfumes have been elusive outside Piedmont, but I am sure that someone some day will manage to capture them.

Two more Piedmontese reds

Piedmont is also the home of two more definitively Italian grape varieties: Barbera and Dolcetto.

Barbera produces much lighter wines that are noticeably high in acidity rather than tannin. Unoaked Barbera has for long been the everyday wine of the Piedmontese who would drink them young, sometimes slightly chilled, and with a completely different frame of mind than that required for the great Nebbiolo. Recently, however, there has been a trend to treat Barbera more seriously and give it wood aging and a bit of bottle-age potential. These wines can be some of the best-value introductions to Piedmont's delicious reds.

Dolcetto is even more frivolous and gulpable though not sweet, despite the name. It is dry, very fruity, and quite sweet because it is low in acidity (certainly relative to Barbera). Dolcetto should generally be drunk within a year or two of the vintage.

Sangiovese in all its forms

The other great red wine grape of Italy is Sangiovese, named after Saint Jove. It is grown all over central Italy and produces wines of extremely varied quality, but is notably responsible for all the great classic wines of Tuscany: Brunello di Montalcino, Vino Nobile de Montepulciano, Chianti Classico, and many more.

Sangiovese is one of those grapes of which many different clones have been planted, with widely varying results. The best way initially to come to grips with "typical" Sangiovese is to taste a well-made Chianti, probably a Chianti Classico from the heartland of the Chianti region. Much of the Sangiovese planted in the Chianti region ripens late and produces quite pale wines (particularly if, as was once common, some local white Trebbiano grapes are also blended in), although there is an extensive program of replanting with better-quality, deeper-colored clones. Other characteristics of Sangiovese are marked acidity and a certain rustic flavor.

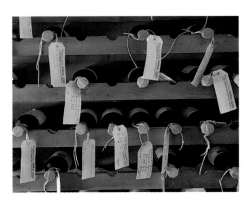

My tasting notes for Chiantis are littered with the word "farmyardy"—though I like them a lot. As with so many Italian reds, there is

CHIANTI CLASSICO
RISERVA, CHIANTI AT
ITS MOST LONG-LIVED.

also often the suggestion of bitterness. The main distinguishing marks of a Sangiovese-based Chianti are therefore: ruby, with some hint of orange after only three or four years; a smell of old vegetation; lots of acidity; some bitterness and a certain graininess of texture. But as Chianti Classico Riserva, Sangiovese becomes an intense, noble, ageworthy wine with real savor.

Sangiovese is grown all over Romagna and Umbria as well as Tuscany. Its most ordinary manifestation is tart, pale red inexpensive Sangiovese di Romagna that should be drunk as young as possible and is made from the least toothsome clones of Sangiovese persuaded to yield at very high levels. (Though Romagna does have some fine quality clones of Sangiovese, too.)

Chianti

Any Italian specialist retailer should stock a good selection of Chiantis. The Chianti region is constantly evolving. Chianti Classico is more concentrated and worth aging than most straight Chiantis, and its badge of office is a black cockerel and seal on the back of the brown straight-sided bottle. Try to make your own palate picture of the Sangiovese. Note the relative bitterness, high acid, and an intriguing knit of different elements in the nose.

A good quality-assessment exercise would be to try to distinguish blind between an inexpensive Sangiovese di Romagna and a fairly young Chianti Classico. There should be much more flavor in the more expensive wine to illustrate what the other lacks. There are hundreds of estates, but the reliable wines of Antinori are easy to find.

Sangiovese plus Cabernet Sauvignon

Sangiovese reaches its most famous and expensive peak in Brunello di Montalcino, made around the town of Montalcino exclusively from a strain of Sangiovese Grosso known as Brunello. These wines have a mass, substance, and aging potential in an altogether different class from Chianti. Nearby Montepulciano has its own "Vino Nobile" also made from a locally adapted strain of Sangiovese and Vino Nobile di Montepulciano can sometimes be almost as majestic as Brunello.

In the Chianti region there has been a similar sort of revolution to that in Piedmont. Some of the more progressive producers

SANGIOVESE VINES
FOR BRUNELLO DI
MONTALCINO.

successfully fought for a reduction in the amount of white grapes that is officially required in the blend, and nowadays many of them omit Trebbiano (that was only ever written into the laws because there was a surplus of it and it is particularly easy to grow). Some use small oak cooperage as in Bordeaux, an alternative to the much bigger Slovenian oak casks traditionally used. This tends to produce more elegant, less rustic wines capable of longer life and well suited to subsequent bottle-aging. Antinori were pioneers of this and their Tignanello was the prototype "Supertuscan," a non-classic great wine from Tuscany—in this case representing the effects of small oak, no white grapes, and the addition of up to 10 percent Cabernet Sauvignon to the traditional Chianti blend. Now much copied, it is a fascinating example of the power this Bordeaux grape has to shape flavor even in small quantities. Also in Tuscany, the 250-year-old tradition of adding up to 10 percent Cabernet to the Carmignano blend demonstrates that this has made sense for years.

Other examples of Cabernet's invasion of Italy are Sassicaia, grown on the Tuscan coast from 100 percent Cabernet Sauvignon and given similar cellar treatment to Tignanello, and the fabulously priced Solaia from hillside vineyards. This wine shows that Italy is eminently capable of producing delicious wines from imported grapes, though you will probably find it easy to distinguish it from a red Bordeaux. Nowadays, Tuscan producers are more likely to value top-quality Sangiovese just as highly as Cabernet Sauvignon—a reflection of an international trend to re-evaluate local strengths rather than to persist in the belief that everything imported from France must be superior.

More red grapes

Tempranillo—an Iberian treasure

Tempranillo is Spain's noblest red grape variety and plays the leading role in its two most famous red wines, Rioja and Ribera del Duero (a relatively recent star).

Its name comes from *temprano,* or "early," and it does ripen relatively early, making it suitable for such high-altitude vineyards as

**TEMPRANILLO VINES
IN RIOJA, ITS ORIGINAL
STRONGHOLD.**

Ribera del Duero (where it is known as Tinto Fino, or fine dark one) and the west of Rioja, the Rioja Alta and Rioja Alavesa. It is also grown in Navarra, in Penedes as Ull de Llebre and farther south in Valdepeñas as Cencibel. Widely grown in Portugal, down river of Ribera del Duero, on the bank of the river the Portuguese call the Douro, in port country, the grape is called Tinto Roriz. In the even hotter vineyards of Portugal's Alentejo, it is known as Aragonês.

The trigger words I use for the characteristic flavor of Tempranillo are "tobacco leaf." Even though I have never actually smelled a fresh tobacco leaf, this does the trick for me with its suggestions of both greenness and earthiness and something very definitely savory. The wine produced by Tempranillo tends to be sturdy, deep colored, and capable of aging well. Tempranillo seems to have a natural affinity with oak, traditionally American.

Defining the flavor

An inexpensive, unwooded varietal example of Tempranillo from Navarra such as from Chivite or Palacio de la Vega is probably the best-value way of familiarizing yourself with the scent of Tempranillo—although any Ribera del Duero or Toro would do. Fine Ribera del Duero producers include Alion, Condado de Haza, Pesquera, and Téofilo Reyes.

Touriga Nacional—Portuguese jewel

Portugal produces some very dramatic Tempranillo—though it tends to be faster-maturing than the best Spanish examples. This country is a repository of the most amazing collection of indigenous grape varieties of its own, however. The most obvious high-quality red grape, and one which I am sure will be increasingly planted around the world, is Touriga Nacional, regarded as the best grape for port but also the producer of some very fine table wine, both as a varietal and an ingredient in a blend.

Varietal Touriga Nacional is increasingly bottled in Portugal and is always deep colored, long lived, and hauntingly flavored, with, in good examples, more than a whiff of port about it. Fireworks and deep purple velvet are often suggested by its aroma.

Some of the finest varietal examples are produced by Quinta dos Roques and Quinta da Pellada of Dão.

Pinotage—South Africa's crossing

This crossing of Pinot Noir with Cinsault tastes like neither but has become South Africa's most characteristic red wine. The color is usually a very lively crimson, and the wine is typically ready to drink relatively young, full of lots of round, red fruit flavors and milk chocolate together with, in some less successful cases, a certain hint of household cleaning powder.

Zinfandel—California's own

The origins of this quintessentially California grape were shrouded in mystery until DNA analysis showed it is identical to the Primitivo grape of southern Italy. It ripens unevenly, but can reach extremely high sugar levels, so nowadays porty Zinfandels of 16 percent natural alcohol are by no means unknown—chiefly from ancient low-yielding vines planted before Prohibition. The wine, if grapes are cropped too high, can be simply jammy with rather unappetizingly cloying berry flavors, but in the hands of a good grower and winemaker Zinfandel can be an extremely noble wine—a claret style worthy of wood aging, even if it usually reaches its best within five to eight years of the vintage. The Sierra Foothills have some particularly ancient Zinfandel vines.

Some of the best Zinfandels are made by Ridge Vineyards, Ravenswood (vineyard-designated bottlings), and Renwood. Martinelli's Jackass Hill and Turley Cellars' output are famous examples of the high-alcohol style.

So-called white Zinfandel is usually a waste of red grapes—a pale pink wine made from underripe Zinfandel (and, often, other more aromatic grapes to add flavor).

CENTURY-OLD ZINFANDEL VINES IN SONOMA, CALIFORNIA, WITH SPRING COVER CROP OF MUSTARD.

Malbec—so much better in Argentina

The Malbec grape is most famous in France for the still somewhat rustic wines of Cahors in the southwest of the country. Sometime last century, cuttings were taken to Argentina and so obviously thrived there that Malbec became the country's most widely planted and consistently successful red grape variety. Under the hot South American sun, in the irrigated vineyards of Mendoza in particular (just over the Andes from Chile's wine country), Malbec produces wines that are full of extract and drama with a sort of silky richness that is entirely lacking in any Cahors that has yet come my way.

Defining the taste

Get your hands on a bottle of Argentine Malbec. This should not be too difficult since Argentina is one of the world's biggest wine producers. There is almost as much consistency between producers of this as there is of Chilean Cabernet, although Cadus and Catena Alta are particularly concentrated. Notice the high alcohol, acidity that, if it is notable, has probably been added, and remarkable extract (the wine tastes "thick"). In fact, some ultra-ripe, high-alcohol examples of Argentine Malbec can be downright syrupy.

Some common red blends

Bordeaux and similar wines elsewhere, including North American Meritage-style wines: Cabernet Sauvignon, Merlot, Cabernet Franc

Rhône and similar wines elsewhere: Syrah, Grenache, Mourvèdre

Rioja and Navarra: Tempranillo, Garnacha (Grenache Noir)

Central Italy: Sangiovese, the local Canaiolo, Colorino plus possibly Trebbiano (bad) or a little Cabernet Sauvignon or Merlot (often good)

Australia and Provence: Cabernet Sauvignon, Shiraz/Syrah

Advanced tasting:
Bordeaux versus Burgundy

Here is an exercise so important it deserves a section all to itself. Outsiders might think that telling red Bordeaux from red Burgundy is absurdly simple—until you have blindfolded them and proved they can't even tell red from white. One friend of mine marked her newly won status as Master of Wine by identifying a Burgundy as a Bordeaux at the celebratory dinner. The longest-living British wine merchant Harry Waugh offered comfort to us all with his reply when asked when he had last mistaken Bordeaux for Burgundy. "Oh, not since lunch," he smiled.

You can do this exercise with any red Bordeaux and Burgundy, though it makes sense to choose a pair of roughly the same age and quality. Any of the wines suggested so far would do; your example of standard Cabernet Sauvignon and Pinot Noir would make a particularly good pair. On page 167 is a crude outline of your deductions in the order you're likely to make them.

THIS WINE LOOKS DEEP
ENOUGH TO BE CABERNET
SAUVIGNON, BUT NOT SO
BLUE THAT IT IS
PARTICULARLY YOUNG.

Interpreting the clues

Color	pale suggests Pinot, or Cab in poor year	deep suggests Cab, or Pinot in very good year
Viscosity	low suggests Pinot	high suggests Cab or heavily chaptalized Pinot
Flavor	raspberries/vegetables mean Pinot	blackcurrants and/or cedar/herbaceous mean Cabernet
Sweetness	sweet suggests Pinot, or Cab in opulent year	dry suggests Cabernet
Acidity	marked suggests Pinot, or very young (or ancient) Cab	swamped by fruit suggests Cabernet
Tannin	low suggests Pinot, or very mature Cabernet	high suggests youthful Cab
Body	light suggests Pinot, or very poor Cab	full suggests Cab, or Pinot from an exceptional vintage

Note that it helps here, as so often, to have an accomplice to feed you an unidentified glass of each. It is wise to keep the glasses in the same relation to each other, so that your accomplice knows that the glass on the left, say, is always the red Bordeaux. Or the accomplice can mark the glasses with a felt-tip pen. If you have (or prefer) to perform this feat solo, you can do it by switching the glasses round and round so that eventually you forget which is which. The trouble is that you can't top up your glass in the middle of the exercise, and you need to have learned enough to be able to match each glass to the contents of the bottles when the exercise is over.

If you can master this classic test of wine expertise, you should be justly proud of yourself. Now you could try to distinguish between a St. Emilion or Pomerol and a red Burgundy. The Merlot-based wine will also have sweetness, but it is a plummy sort of richness in a full-bodied tannic wine with lots of color, whereas red Burgundies are more likely to offer a raspberry sort of fruitiness in a wine that is lighter in both color and body.

Bordeaux—a geography lesson

Bordeaux is a very large and obligingly well-ordered wine region, which is why it is such a favorite with those who enjoy blind tasting.

Bordeaux is divided into separate estates or châteaux which don't change (or not that much) from year to year. Each region—Médoc, Graves, St. Emilion, Pomerol, and the lesser ones—is divided into neat communes or parishes, each of which should have their own characteristics just as each vintage puts its own stamp on to the wines it produces. This is particularly true in the region that produces Bordeaux's biggest quantity of top-quality wine, the Médoc (although it is under threat from the current trend to produce all red wines as big, deep, and alcoholic as possible, thereby blurring the differences between communes).

When tasting a red Bordeaux blind, you should first of all decide whether you are faced with primarily Merlot (St. Emilion/Pomerol) or Cabernet Sauvignon (Médoc/Graves). If you smell the rich plumminess of Merlot, look for great intense spiciness that suggests lots of it—with a deep color—and that would lead you to Pomerol. If the Merlot seems to have been mixed with a noticeable proportion of aromatic Cabernet Franc, producing a slightly lighter wine with a whiff of barely roasted beef about it, then this would suggest stereotypical St. Emilion.

In a wine that seems to made of predominantly Cabernet Sauvignon, look for the distinctive "texture," a sort of dry, sandy, almost earthy taste that is characteristic of Graves. If you don't find it, you should in theory start trying to work out which of the Médoc communes the wine could come from. (In practice, most blind tasters are casting about wildly by this stage. Could be Italy? California perhaps?)

The Médoc communes

Neatly, the most northerly commune, St. Estèphe, typically produces the wines highest in acidity. Wines from St. Estèphe have been stereotypically hard and very tannic when young.

Pauillac is the most famous commune, with three of the four Médoc "first growths" classified in 1855. Its wines tend to be very concentrated and blackcurrant with lots of tannin.

Margaux is quite a way to the south and wines made there tend to be more delicate, fragrant, and slightly more Merlot-y.

St. Julien contains lots of second-growth châteaux and, typically, makes wines that come somewhere between Pauillac and Margaux—"just enough of everything" is the convenient description, though a certain cedarwood flavor is associated with the commune.

This amount of detail is given here because Bordeaux guessing games are the most common and can, believe it or not, be great fun. I suspect that those who indulge in them have more faith than I in just how likely they are to be right. Remember, it's the getting there that's fun.

Vintage and age

If guessing-the-commune seems a dazzlingly skillful dinner-party trick, guessing-the-vintage assumes almost mystical status.

Contrary to popular belief, there are relatively few sorts of wine in which such a feat makes sense. All the dry, crisp whites we drink with relish when they are young tend to follow the same path toward a stale, unexciting state as the years pass, so that guessing the vintage for many whites equates with guessing the age. The same is true of many of the less exciting reds that are sold in huge volumes to be drunk as young as possible.

Guessing the vintage is significant only for wines that develop interesting characteristics with age, i.e. those that mature rather than simply age, and are made in regions where the weather varies sufficiently from year to year to give each vintage its own character. This means that in practice vintage-guessing is a widespread exercise only for white wines based on Chardonnay, Riesling, and Sémillon and reds from the classic grape varieties discussed in this chapter. It is with red Bordeaux, again, that most fun can be had with vintage guessing. California Cabernets do vary from vintage to vintage, but the much more temperate climate of Bordeaux fashions the most dramatic vintage variations.

There is no shortage of literature in magazines and newsletters on the characteristics of different vintages and how they are evolving. It is important to realize, by the way, that as wines develop in the bottle, the way different vintages are regarded also evolves. The 1991 vintage was rather overlooked in Burgundy chiefly because it followed a run of three extremely good vintages but, as I write in 2000, this is the vintage that is arguably giving the most pleasure of all to Burgundy drinkers.

Comparing consecutive vintages

However, it is worth studying a specific example of just how different two consecutive vintages can be. We have seen that red wines lose color and start to go brown with age, but there is much more to identifying Bordeaux vintages than guessing age. The 1991 vintage, for instance, was a poor, thin thing compared with 1990. Looking at a 1991 red Bordeaux compared with a 1990, you might be tempted to think it was older, so pale will it be in comparison. Look at the actual hue. The 1990 is probably quite a bit more developed, or orangey, at the rim. When you taste the 1991 next to the 1990, you will see that it is much lighter in body and interest. The 1990 wine is much more concentrated in both color and flavor, often still with noticeable tannin.

Stages of growth

Remember that with red wines, tannin, blueish tints, and depth of color are all indications of youth, while complexity of flavor and fading of hue suggest maturity. If you have bought a quantity of the same wine, a case of a dozen bottles for instance, you will want to monitor its progress so that you don't drink it too soon. With a moderate-quality red Bordeaux, the wine might be ready to drink within three to five years of the vintage, while the most revered names can take three decades to mature. Generally speaking, the better the wine, the longer you will have to wait before it can prove it. The sadness is, of course, that you can never know when a wine has reached its peak of quality until it has passed it. Again in general terms, Cabernet Sauvignon, Syrah, and Nebbiolo wines take longer to mature than those based on Merlot, Cabernet Franc, Pinot Noir, Grenache, Sangiovese, Zinfandel, and Pinotage. Top-quality Tempranillo and Touriga Nacional can take some time to mature, but early-drinking examples are also made.

Also bear in mind that many wines, especially fine reds, go through a "dumb" stage, during which it does not say much to your senses, particularly your nose. Especially when recently bottled, about two years after the vintage and/or at certain periods over the next decade or so, good-quality reds can seem very closed up, as though they are turning in on themselves to concentrate on knitting together all the elements inside the bottle. Don't write off a wine that is very deep colored and tannic but without much bouquet. If it is youthful it may well be getting ready to reveal its charms.

Age of the vine

The age of the vines plays an important part in determining the flavor of the wine they produce.

In quantitative terms the vine starts producing a sensible amount of wine in its third year and reaches a peak at about fifteen to twenty years, then decreases steadily so that at fifty years it is scarcely economic to cultivate such an aged plant. The quality of the wine produced tends to increase with age, however, so that really dedicated winemakers search out very old vines, however uneconomic their crop, to add depth and complexity of flavor to their blends—or even to make special wines exclusively from old vine fruit.

Although a vine's first commercial crop can be particularly good quality (perhaps because the fruit-to-leaf ratio is relatively high at this stage), in general, wines made from ancient vines have

many more layers of flavor. Try to compare wines such as Zinfandel that are available in old vine form and regular form and see what you think, although some agree it is not the age of the vine but simply the crop load that is the determining factor.

SERIOUSLY OLD ZINFANDEL VINES IN SONOMA'S RUSSIAN RIVER, PLANTED WELL BEFORE PROHIBITION.

Old and young

Seek out examples of wines that are available in two similar forms, one from young vines or vines for which no claim of age is made, and one from old vines, which should be indicated on the label by the words *vieilles vignes* in French, *cepas velhas* in Portuguese or *alte Reben* in German, for example. Compare the depth of flavor, and even the color in each.

Different vineyard sites

In a sense, all fine wine tasting proves the extraordinary point that different vineyard sites, even adjacent ones, produce wines of quite different character.

On a frosty morning, take a good look any plot of land—field, garden, or backyard. Notice how much thicker the frost is in some parts of it. Alternatively, monitor a similar plot of land during a particularly hot day. Notice how natural features generally protect some parts of it from this searing heat and expose others. This is visible evidence of the variability of physical above-ground environments. And when you add the fact that soils and subsoils tend to vary enormously below the ground, it is not surprising that each vineyard tends to have its own physical character, what the French call *terroir*, which it impresses on the wine made from it.

Vineyard and wine

To demonstrate (though not necessarily explain) the phenomenon to yourself, taste any two wines made by the same producer from the same vintage in the same area but carrying different vineyard designations. This could be two Burgundies, two Bordeaux Châteaux within the same commune, or two nearby vineyard-designated wines from Australia or California. You could use the invaluable *World Atlas of Wine* (Mitchell Beazley) as a guide. I can think of no better example than a range of wines from the great Mosel winemaker J. J. Prüm. Wines from the adjacent Wehlener Sonnenuhr and Graacher Himmelreich vineyard sites clearly show how much more sunshine the former attracts simply because it is oriented a few more degrees toward the sun on the banks of the river.

Bottle size

Wines kept in different size bottles typically mature at different rates; while they all contain roughly the same amount of oxygen, that oxygen acts on very different volumes of wine.

Half-bottles encourage the wines to mature rapidly, but perhaps without picking up quite such interest along the way as a standard bottle size. Reckoned to be most satisfactory of all is the magnum, containing 1.5 liters or two standard bottles. This is why a magnum of fine wine usually costs more than two standard bottles. Even bigger bottles are often sold, but more for their novelty value—especially the giant Champagne bottles; the champagne is usually not matured in that bottle; the bottle is filled, under pressure, from several smaller bottles.

Large and small
Hunt down a wine at least three or four years old that is available in both whole and half-bottles and compare how each tastes. The wine in the half-bottle will probably look older (browner) and taste more developed and less tannic (if the wine is red) and less tart (if the wine is white).

WINE IS GENERALLY BOTTLED IN SIZES CONTAINING 1.5 LITERS, 75CL, 50CL (ESPECIALLY FOR SWEET WHITES), 37.5CL AND (FOR AIRLINES ETC.) 18.75CL.

5. Strong and sparkling wines

How the bubbles
get in the bottle

Wine is made to sparkle in several different ways. The most laborious and expensive method, predictably, makes the best-quality wine.

This is the traditional method, or *méthode traditionnelle*, and is the way champagne (the name reserved in most of the world for the sparkling wines of the Champagne region in northeast France) and the best California fizz, is made. It is based on the fact that carbon dioxide gas is given off during fermentation. Carefully selected base wine is put into strong bottles with a little sugar and yeast and stoppered up. The yeast acts on the sugar to provoke a second fermentation in bottle, which gives off some gas, kept in solution in that bottle, and also leaving some sediment. It is the interaction between this sediment and the base wine (called yeast autolysis) that is responsible for the special taste of really good sparkling wine. The longer that the wine lies in contact with this sediment, the more complex the flavor—and there is precious little effect at all at under eighteen months.

The only problem—a purely cosmetic one—is that we like our sparkling wines to be crystal clear rather than besmirched by any sediment. So when the wine is ready to be sold, the bottles are gradually upended, and the sediment is shaken into the

THE ORIGINAL LABOR-
INTENSIVE WAY OF SHAKING
THE SEDIMENT INTO THE
BOTTLENECK IS CALLED
REMUAGE IN FRENCH.

bottleneck either by hand or machine. The bottlenecks are then frozen and opened under pressure so that the sediment flies out as a frozen pellet, to be topped up by some more wine and, usually, a little sugar, called the "dosage." The driest wines are called "Brut"; some are even extra Brut as they have no dosage at all. Extra Dry is actually slightly sweeter than Brut.

The bubbles produced by this traditional method tend to be smaller, steadier, and more long-lasting than by any other method. Wines made this way will usually have (French) "champagne," "traditional method," or "fermented in this bottle" on the label. At the other end of the scale, there is the straightforward "bicycle pump" method whereby gas is simply pumped into generally cheap base wine, just as carbonated sodas and colas are made fizzy. These, the most basic sparkling wines, tend to start off with a great fizz of big bubbles but go flat quite quickly.

In-between these two extremes is the most common method—the tank or Charmat method—relying on the so-called *cuve close* or sealed tank. This way a second fermentation is encouraged in a tank rather than a bottle so that the same sort of gas is produced, but there is much less useful contact between most of the wine and the sediment. The wine is then bottled under pressure.

There is also the transfer method, denoted by the words "bottled fermented" or "fermented in bottle" on the label, whereby a second fermentation is provoked in the bottle, but then the wine is emptied out of the bottle, filtered, and then rebottled—all while under pressure.

Cheap fizz

In a well-stocked pub or wine bar, order a glass apiece of the establishment's cheapest sparkling wine, one that makes no claims about how it was made on the label, and its most expensive champagne. Compare the size of the bubbles and notice how the champagne retains its fizz much longer than the cheaper version.

WITH BUBBLES IN WINE, THE SMALLER THE BETTER.

CHAMPAGNE CELLARS, LIKE VEUVE CLICQUOT'S, ARE OFTEN HEWN
OUT OF THE LOCAL CHALK.

The blending recipe

*Champagne, and virtually all of the best sparkling wines, are made
from a carefully composed blend of ingredients. Chardonnay, Pinot
Noir, a less intense cousin called Pinot Meunier, and occasionally Pinot
Blanc are almost invariably the favored grapes.*

A wine made exclusively from Chardonnay is called a Blanc de
Blancs and one from dark-skinned Pinot grapes only is a Blanc de
Noirs, but most are a blend. The Pinot grapes are pressed so gently
before fermentation that the resultant wine is quite pale. The ideal
base wine, as in brandy, is quite tart and neutral and the champagne
blender's art is to predict how such a blend will turn out after the
second fermentation and all that time spent aging on the sediment.
Cheaper sparkling wines tend to be made of much cheaper grapes.

The Champagne region is virtually at the northern-most limit
of cultivation (although some fine counterparts have been made in
England). This means that the wines are naturally high in acidity,
which can only be satisfactorily counterbalanced by mellowing time
spent on that sediment. The quick-fix way adopted by makers of
cheap champagne is to age the wine for the legal minimum (15
months) and then bottle it with a high dosage. This horrid, jagged
mix of sugar and acidity is usually made all the nastier by the fact
that the cheapest grapes in champagne are those that have been
heavily pressed—so the wine is astringent to boot. Cheap
champagne can be a very nasty drink; good-quality sparkling wine
from elsewhere is usually much more attractive—and no more
expensive than cheap champagne.

theory

What's in the price?

Compare the taste of a fine champagne made with the best grapes with a much cheaper one. Is there not a much deeper, richer, more biscuity flavor in the more expensive wine?

What's in a name?

Compare, the next time you have to entertain in quantity, a bottle of the cheapest French champagne you can find with some of the finest sparkling wines made directly in its image elsewhere in the world. Moët et Chandon's outposts

Domaine Chandon in California and Australia are obvious candidates for this exercise. Roederer Estate, an American offshoot of the Champagne house Louis Roederer, is probably the best producer of California sparkling wine. Croser is another fine fizzy Aussie, and Pelorus, made by the Cloudy Bay team, is a good example from New Zealand. You will probably find the New World example much easier to drink and much less tart and astringent than the cheap champagne.

All that sparkles...

Sparkling wine is made virtually everywhere that wine is made, but these are some of the most important types of fizz:

Cava: the extremely popular Spanish version made mainly in Catalonia from local grapes Macabeo, Xarel-lo and, the finest, Parellada, although Chardonnay and Pinot Noir are increasingly common. These wines tend to be particularly frothy, and often have a dense lemony flavor to them that is quite different from the creaminess of a Pinot/Chardonnay blend.

Talento: Italy's traditional method (*metodo classico*) fizz made mainly from Chardonnay and Pinot grapes. A speciality of Lombardy. Ca del Bosco reigns.

Crémant de Loire: made from Chenin Blanc and some Chardonnay grapes in the Loire. This can often be very fine, more delicate, and slightly sweeter-tasting than champagne and definitely different.

Sekt: wine made fizzy any old way in Germany and Austria. If the base wine was German (relatively rare) it is called Deutscher Sekt, but aromatic grapes like Riesling result in a very different, lighter style of wine.

Serving fizz

A bottle of sparkling wine may signify celebration but is also a potentially dangerous weapon.

The gas is stored inside the bottle at about the same pressure as the tire of very big vehicles. And that pressure can send the cork flying with such speed that it can do a great deal of damage, especially to the human eye. Always hold the cork down with your thumb or palm until it gently eases out of the bottleneck.

Keeping your thumb over the top of the cork at all times, untwist the wire muzzle that holds down the cork and ease it off. Then, still keeping the cork in the bottleneck, gently twist the bottle off the cork, holding the bottle at a 45 degree angle to maximize the surface area of the wine and minimize the pressure under the cork. If you are doing your job properly the cork should come out of the bottle slowly with a gentle sigh, and not a loud pop. The colder the wine (fizzy wines can take being chilled rather more severely than most white wines) and the less it has recently been shaken about, the easier it will be to achieve this. In short, the traditional champagne opening ceremony that racing drivers enjoy after winning a race is an object lesson in how not to open a bottle of fizz.

Because bubbles are the point of sparkling wine, it is worth serving it in a glass that preserves these for as long as possible, i.e. a tall, thin one (not a saucer). To get the most from the flavor, choose champagne glasses that go in a little toward the rim.

Fizziness, or the "mousse" as it is called by professionals, is particularly sensitive to traces of dish detergent, so take care that champagne glasses are rinsed with special care.

Washing up

With some relatively inexpensive sparkling wine, experiment with two glasses, one of which has been rinsed much more carefully than the other and notice how much less fizzy is the wine in the less rinsed glass.

Sherry—the insider's wine

Sherry is a bit like fine German wine—enormously appreciated by wine professionals and virtually ignored by the general wine-drinking public, with the result that much of it is dramatically underpriced.

Sherry is what is known as a fortified wine, i.e. a wine that has been fortified by the addition of spirit—neutral grape brandy. In the case of sherry (unlike port), the spirit is always added to a dry, fully fermented wine.

Most sherry comes from near the Andalucian town of Jerez de la Frontera (which inspired its name) in southern Spain. It is made mainly from the Palomino grape, which comes into its own here.

Sherry—defining the taste The Palomino grape naturally produces the following wide range of styles, all of which are tangy and bone dry:

Fino
Pale, light (maybe 15.5 percent alcohol), an excellent aperitif and appetite-whetter, especially in hot weather.

Manzanilla
Effectively a Fino produced in the seaside town of Sanlúcar de Barrameda, west of Jerez and therefore supposedly slightly salty, too.

Amontillado
An aged Fino that takes on a deep tawny color and many layers of flavor after years in wooden casks (butts). Also nutty and contains about 17.5 percent alcohol. This can be a great winter aperitif, and goes well with soups.

Oloroso
Even richer, fuller, and nuttier than an Amontillado. A Dry Oloroso is what the Jerezanos drink when they're not sloshing down Fino. It is delicious with nuts and cheese.

Palo Cortado
A rare style that is a particularly intriguing cross between an Amontillado and an Oloroso.

MORE CHALK—DAZZLINGLY WHITE VINEYARDS IN SHERRY COUNTRY.

All of these are very fine wines, almost invariably made from a "solera" in which lots of different ages of sherry are routinely and fractionally blended, so vintage-dated sherry is very rare. But the good name of sherry has been sullied over the years by the sustained and apparently popular fashion for sweetening up blends of very ordinary wines for the big-selling commercial brands and calling them Amontillado, Oloroso, or, when a great deal of sweetening has been added, Cream. (Pale Cream is one that has had the color bleached out of it.) Such wines are to real sherry as Liebfraumilch is to a fine, estate-bottled Mosel.

Tasting the difference
Find a bottle or half-bottle (good sherry is often sold in halves) of an Amontillado or Oloroso sold as (Very) Dry, or (Muy) Seco. Taste it and then compare it with a commercial brand. Tilt the two glasses away from you against a white background and compare the hue at the rim. See how the commercial one has none of the yellow-green hue suggesting great age and how it is not only much sweeter, but tastes far less distinguished, muddier, and soupier than the superior sherry.

There are some fine sweeter sherries, generally made by adding dried Pedro Ximénez grapes to blends of seriously old, dry wines. Such wines can be delicious accompaniments to many desserts and Gonzalez Byass's Matusalem is one of the best. See page 192 for further specifically recommended sherries.

Port—the strongest wine

This is a popular fortified wine and is one of the sweetest examples of red wine. True port is from northern Portugal, but the style is widely copied.

Port is made by adding grape spirit to sweet, fermenting must before the fermentation is finished. This stops the fermentation process because yeast can't work at very high levels of alcohol, so the result is strong (almost 20 percent alcohol) and therefore sweet.

White port, made from pale-skinned grapes, is drunk as an aperitif in the rugged Douro Valley in northern Portugal.

VINTAGE PORT IS ONE OF THE LONGEST-LASTING WINES OF ALL—THOUGH ITS IMAGE HAS BEEN GETTING LESS DUSTY.

Types of port
Basically port is red, strong, and sweet and comes in the following different styles:

Ruby
The youngest sort of "wood port" (port that has been matured only in the cask rather than the bottle). A lively, straightforward young port.

Tawny
A much gentler, subtler style of wood port that has been aged for much longer in the cask until it takes on a tawny hue and is labeled as a 10, 20, 30, or Over 40 year old, or a much cheaper commercial one that is basically made tawny by blending some white port with a young ruby. Sandeman's 20-year-old is good.

Vintage
Relatively rare but the smartest sort of port in existence, made only in the finest years—about one in every three. A carefully selected blend of the finest young ports bottled scarcely two years after the harvest and left preferably for decades—ideally at least one—to mature in bottle. All the sediment that falls to the bottom of the cask when maturing a Tawny therefore develops in the bottle, which is why vintage port, unlike wood ports, should be decanted.

LBV
Stands for Late Bottled Vintage and is a bit of a misnomer. These are ports of a quality either just or decidedly below that of vintage, which are blended and bottled between four and six years after the vintage. The most commercial, and generally cheapest, ones are heavily filtered so that they won't throw a sediment in the bottle, or develop much extra flavor. The better, "proper" LBVs do both and are decidedly superior wines that need decanting.

Single quinta vintage ports
These exciting specimens are made from grapes grown on a single *quinta* (farm) usually, but not necessarily, in years that are not quite good enough to be declared as vintage. They can be very characterful and should also be cellared for some time (not quite as long as a vintage) and decanted.

Superior producers include Dow, Fonseca, Graham, Niepoort, Quinta do Noval, and Taylor.

Defining the taste
Compare a "branded" LBV such as
Noval's with a serious Late Bottled
Vintage port carrying the date of
the vintage on the label. The

second has so much more flavor,
tannin—and sediment.

Young, serious port is wine at its strongest, deepest-colored, and most tannic. Over time it mellows quite miraculously into something smooth and hauntingly multi-layered.

Madeira—buried treasure

This is quintessential Atlantic wine, made exclusively on the steeply terraced vineyards of the Portuguese island of Madeira. Like sherry, madeira does not deserve to be so widely ignored, although it is produced in a much smaller quantity.

Madeira is always refreshingly high in acidity, comes in an array of different sweetness levels, and is about as strong as port. It never throws a sediment in bottle because it is always matured in the cask. It gets its specially warming salt-water-taffy taste from the fact that it is not only fortified and matured in old casks, but is routinely heated during its maturation. This means that an opened bottle of madeira hardly deteriorates at all; a single opened bottle can be enjoyed over several months.

Staying power
Pour a measure of madeira into a
glass (all fortified wines should be
served in smaller glasses, or at
least smaller measures, than table
wines because of their higher
alcohol content). Stand the

madeira next to an equal measure
of table wine in a similar shape
and size of glass and keep going
back to the two glasses over the
hours and days to come. Note how
much faster the table wine
changes, for the worse.

The various styles took their names from the noblest grapes (all white) used traditionally for madeira. The Tinta Negra Mole red grape was widely planted on the island for much of the twentieth century, and is used today for the most commercial styles of madeira.

Types of madeira For the best wines, look for the following terms:

Sercial: the lightest, driest, most searingly acid style of madeira, which, because there is no mitigating sweetness, needs the longest time to mature—a good forty or fifty years ideally!

Verdelho: a tangy grape that produces interesting varietal white table wine in Australia and tangy, medium-dry madeira.

Bual: rich, nutty, medium-sweet madeira, the Oloroso of the island, delicious with cheese and dried fruits.

Malmsey: the sweetest form of madeira, made from a member of the Malvasia family of grapes, which goes particularly well with Christmas cakes and puddings.

Other fortified wines from around the world

Port- and sherry-style wines are made all over the world, notably in South Africa, Australia, and Cyprus. These are some of the other better-known styles:

Australian Muscats and Tokays: fortified like port and aged in hot sheds like madeira; much sweeter and treaclier than either.

Vins Doux Naturels: France makes a host of wines strengthened and sweetened by adding neutral spirit to sweet grape juice. The strong, golden Muscats of Beaumes-de-Venise, Frontignan, Lunel, and St.-Jean-de-Minervois are young grapey examples from the south; Rivesaltes, Banyuls, and Maury of Roussillon are seriously aged and can be porty; Pineau des Charentes and Floc de Gascogne are made from grapes grown in cognac and armagnac country respectively; Ratafia usually comes from Champagne; Macvin from Jura.

Malaga: raisiny syrup from the Costa del Sol that has virtually disappeared.

Marsala: Sicily's answer to madeira; quality is extremely variable.

Vermouth: blend of base wine, alcohol, and usually herby flavorings, often made on an industrial scale.

6. Wine, food, and fun

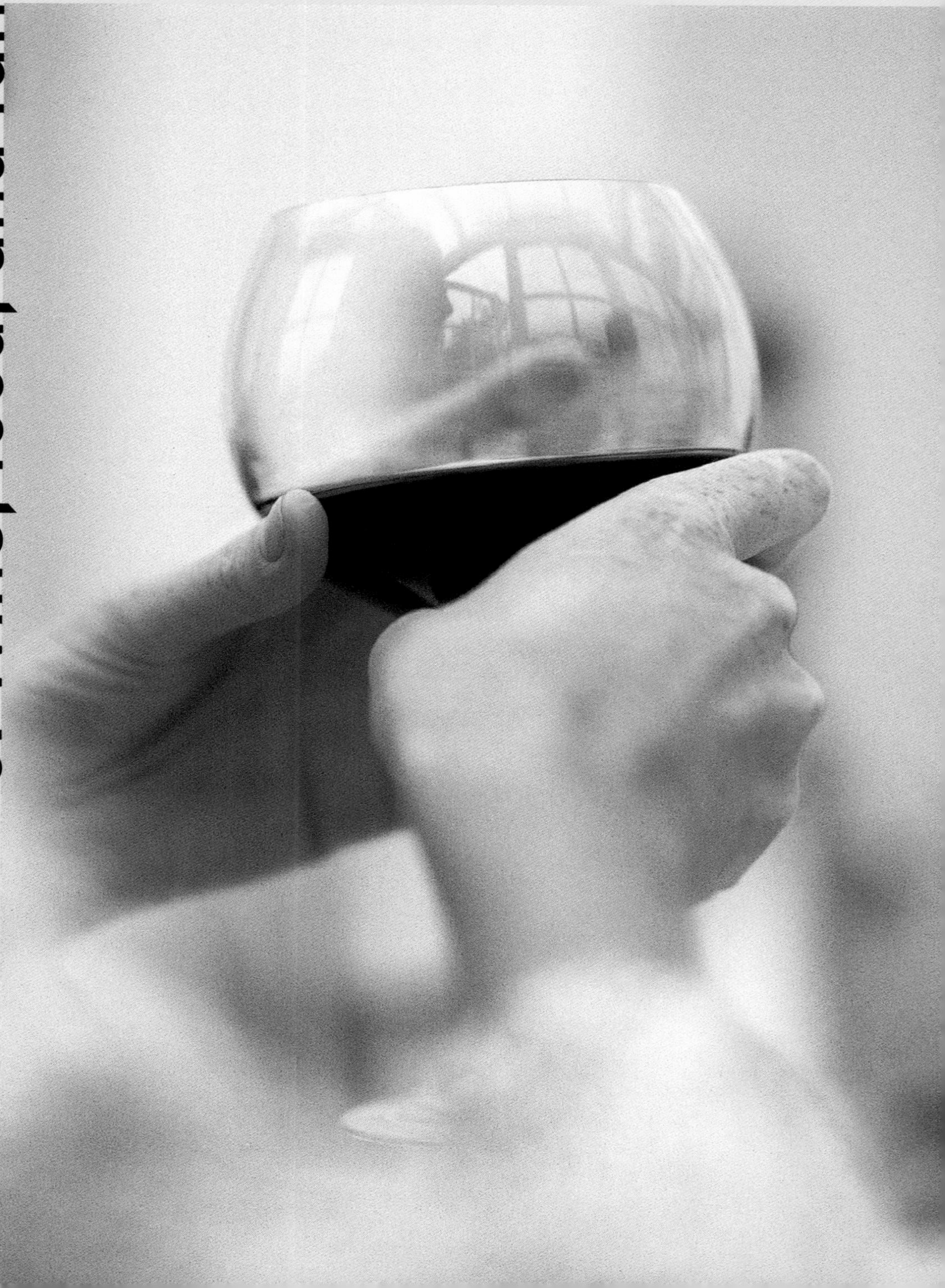

A perfect match

Wine and food make a difficult subject for a book. All the relevant guidelines can either be given in a short chapter such as this, or else it demands a lifetime of research and dissatisfaction.

If you are a purist, you could probably—after many disappointments —find the single wine that would best accompany each food or dish you allowed past your lips. You might match a hearty beef stew, for instance, with Châteauneuf-du-Pape because it too is made up of a maceration of different flavor components. If the stew were to be served with carrots you might choose a wine that depended heavily on the Grenache grape, to complement the sweetness in that vegetable. And if the accompanying potatoes were little new ones, you might be swayed towards a Châteauneuf of recent vintage, while older baked potatoes would suggest a more mature example.

See what I mean? You can let the business of matching solids and liquids get out of hand. In general terms, you can enjoy almost any wine with almost any food. This is particularly true since, in practice, we tend to consume food and drink at discrete intervals. We rarely find ourselves with a mouth of food and wine mixed up together—only if we're feeling particularly greedy. What usually happens is that we consume what is in front of us, or rather we take a selection of the food on our plate and then, when we're feeling thirsty, a mouthful of wine. So long as what we have just eaten doesn't completely destroy our tasting faculties, we can enjoy almost any wine, whatever its character.

In Chapter 2, substances that distract from the business of wine tasting were discussed, and there are a few specific foods that might be served at a meal that would make it more difficult for you to appreciate wine. This is not to say you should never again eat chocolate or mint sauce, simply that it is unwise to serve your guests a very special bottle of wine when at the same time asking them to fill their mouths with such distracting flavors.

The first sip

Next time you're having wine with a meal, notice how you consume the solid and the liquid constituents. You'll probably find that you take a mouthful of the wine before you actually eat anything, which is a very good moment at which to taste it as consciously as possible. Thereafter you use the wine as lubricant for the solid matter you are taking in—just as you would use a glass of water in fact.

Throughout the meal

Try to monitor what effect the food you eat has on the taste of the wine you are drinking. Compare the sensations given by that first mouthful of wine savored before you tasted the food and the mouthful of wine immediately after your first eating session. The food does affect how the wine tastes, doesn't it? If it spoils the wine in any way, just take a mouthful of water before the wine.

Difficult foods for wine

Acids

Anything very high in acidity makes a fine wine a bit difficult to taste afterward (though it can flatter a slightly tart wine). "Buy on an apple and sell on cheese" is an old wine-trade adage, illustrating the flattering nature of cheese—it softens the palate and makes it ready for a gulp of wine—and the much less flattering effects of the acidity in apples on wine tasted immediately afterward. Some

WITH THEIR RUBBERY TEXTURE, SOFT CHEESES CAN BE MORE DIFFICULT PARTNERS FOR WINE THAN HARD ONES (SEE PAGE 197).

acids seem kinder on wine than others. A squeeze of lemon juice is not going to ruin a wine, but a particularly sharp vinegar is no fun for any wine—or any palate for that matter.

Artichoke

Globe artichoke has a strange taste that makes wine taste metallic. It contains an odd compound, dubbed cynarin, that makes great wine wasted on the magnificent globe. It has so much liquid in it that you probably won't want any lubrication anyway.

Asparagus

Almost the same applies as for globe artichokes, though Sauvignon Blanc can tackle asparagus.

Egg yolk

A soft yolk seems to coat and bind the mouth and leaves your taste buds defenseless and dulled. You may need some bread between mouthfuls to clean your palate.

Chocolate

Very similar effect to soft yolks—again, in part, because of its texture. A lightly chocolate-flavored mousse might not play havoc with your palate but a bar of chocolate would. Note, however, that a wine served with any sweet food has to be even sweeter than that food—which can be difficult with some particularly indulgent chocolate desserts.

Kippers

These smoked herrings are very oily and salty. I suspect it is the oiliness that prevents you from properly savoring a wine, for much the same reason as egg yolks and chocolate are barred from the company of fine-for-wine foods. These and other very oily foods seem best countered with a fruity or very tannic wine.

Mint

Just as peppermints are not the best preparation for a wine tasting, very minty puddings or salads and (especially) a mint sauce that combines mint with vinegar will make a pretty poor accompaniment to fine wine.

Spices

Subtly spiced dishes can be lovely partners for fairly full-bodied or even slightly sweet wines, but a vindaloo or really hot chilli, it must be admitted, is not great with wine. Your mouth is left stinging and in no shape to measure the acidity, sweetness, etc., of a wine. You can still "nose" a wine, but even your nasal passages are likely to have been heated up by the spice.

Taste for yourself

ACIDITY AND WINE

Take some wine that you don't value too highly—or preferably two of very different styles, one light-bodied white and one full-bodied red. Now try the wines before and after mouthfuls of the following, all high in different sorts of acidity:

lemon juice (citric acid)
vinegar (acetic acid)
natural yogurt (lactic acid).

Monitor how much each affects the flavor of the wine, making sure that your mouth is well rinsed in each substance. Notice how much more acid the wine tastes after the vinegar, though less markedly so after the lemon juice and yogurt. Might this suggest a modification to your salad dressings when serving wine? Notice too that the lighter-bodied wine is more affected. Strong-flavored, full-bodied wines don't seem to mind the acid distractions too much. Now try the apple and cheese trick. See how different a wine tastes after each—especially a young wine, the sort that was most frequently bought and sold and therefore gave rise to the adage.

ARTICHOKES AND ASPARAGUS AND WINE

Next time you're eating artichoke or asparagus, try out this surprising theory about wine taken with them. Don't you find your mouth left with a distinctly un-winey flavor if you try to drink wine just after a mouthful of either vegetable? Even water tastes a bit odd—slightly metallic—after a mouthful of artichoke.

EGG AND WINE

Egg yolks are probably the least serious offenders in keeping you from wine-inspired pleasure. Nevertheless, try a glass of red wine with your next soft-boiled egg and notice how difficult it is to taste the wine properly.

CHOCOLATE AND WINE

Can you really judge a mouthful of wine after one of chocolate? Incidentally, few of these tricky foods impair your smelling or "nosing" abilities. You can still get most of the flavor of the wine, but you can't judge aspects such as sweetness, acidity, and tannin properly, for which the inside of your mouth needs to be in prime, unsullied tasting condition.

KIPPERS AND WINE

Tea and kippers are made for each other. Prove it by trying kippers with wine instead of tea.

MINTS AND WINE

After-dinner mints are double-killers of wine, of course. Don't eat them till you know you don't want any more wine—though a very rich port would probably force its way through the menthol and smear of cocoa butter.

SPICES AND WINE

With curries, chilled beer can be deliciously refreshing, but if you really want to drink grape rather than grain, try the full-bodied, dry, but rather spicy wines of Alsace. You'll probably want something refreshingly cool, but it will need lots of body weight to stand up to the spice.

Cleansing your palate

There is a simple solution to the tricky problem of eating unsuitable food and enjoying wine at the same time. You can swiftly neutralize your mouth after a mouthful of food by chewing something bland and absorbent such as bread, or simply swilling around some water in your mouth. You will find that a morsel of bread after a sharply dressed salad or artichoke soon scrubs the mouth clean, ready for a taste of delicious wine.

Bread and wine

After trying any of the "danger" foods listed above, neutralize your mouth with either bread or water and see how much better you can taste the wine afterward. However, curries and mint are too aromatic and will affect the nasal passages as well, so you need more than bread and water—you also need time before you'll be in good wine tasting form again.

Sherry and food

Sherry is the one type of wine that is particularly useful for "difficult" foods because it is full bodied, clean, dry, but forceful enough to stand up to almost any solid. The driest sherries, Fino and Manzanilla, are widely underrated, and indeed underpriced. Because they are very good at stimulating the appetite, they are excellent first-course wines and would go happily with any salad-based dish, eggs, and lots of spicy dishes. Fino with chocolate is not advised, however. Try milk.

A few tips on sherry
Almost any wine shop should have at least one Fino or Manzanilla. Tio Pepe is usually good, as can be La Ina, La Guita Manzanilla, Tres Palmas, and San Patricio. All Finos and Manzanillas should be drunk, chilled, as soon as possible after being bottled and don't last more than a few days in an opened bottle. Half-bottles are therefore useful. Any restaurant that takes sherry seriously obviously takes wine seriously.

THE TRADITIONAL SHERRY GLASS, OR COPITA.

Breaking the rules

So heretically skeptical am I about the business of wine and food that I don't even accept the rule that constitutes most people's knowledge of wine as a subject: white wine with fish and red wine with meat.

I suspect that what gave rise to this adage was the fact that most fish cries out for a bit of acidity to bring out its flavor—lemon juice, capers, and even vinegar are standard accompaniments to fish—and white wines are usually higher in acidity than reds. In fact, this is only marginal. There are lots of red wines that are high in acidity and delicious with fish, especially with fish that is quite strongly flavored and relatively firm, such as tuna, salmon, salmon trout, turbot, John Dory, sea bass, halibut, and brill.

It is true that tannin, in which some red wines are high, does not go happily with delicate flavors of any sort and tends to leave a sort of inky taste if drunk with fish. But light-bodied, low-tannin, high-acid reds such as those cited opposite would be fine with most fish dishes, especially those with a fairly rich sauce. These are wines you could serve cool-ish, too, if you want refreshment.

Red wine and fish   All these red wines should be fine with fish, especially fish that is full in flavor and robust in texture.

Almost any wine made by a version of "carbonic maceration" (and therefore low in tannin) such as Beaujolais, many Côtes-du-Rhône, the lightest Vins de Pays, and juicy young Cabernets.

Most Gamay.

All but the grandest Pinot Noir.

Red Loire wines: Bourgueil, St. Nicolas de Bourgueil, Chinon, Saumur-Champigny, Anjou-Villages.

All but the grandest reds from Germany, Alsace, or Austria.

South Tyrol (Alto Adige) reds.

Bardolino, Valpolicella, most light Italian Cabernets and some Chiantis, unoaked Barbera and Dolcetto.

Red Burgundy from early maturing vintages.

Most red Vins de Pays from the south of France, Coteaux du Tricastin, Côtes de Ventoux, Côtes du Luberon.

Light "clarete-style" Riojas in their youth.

Many New Zealand reds.

And whites with meat
You could take equal enjoyment from any full-bodied white wine—especially Chardonnays, Pinot Gris, and Semillons—with many meat dishes. Again, it is body that matters more than color.

Temperature and weight

Serving temperatures of wine make a difference to how they taste, but the temperature at which you serve food is important, too.

The most obvious thing to bear in mind is that you will not be able to taste anything if you scorch or freeze your mouth. I may sound like an officious nanny, but don't expect to go wine tasting after a piping hot soup. Ice-cold sorbets are none too good, either, I'm afraid, for they have a numbing effect on the inside of your mouth. Best to wait till you have finished eating a sorbet or ice cream before attempting to taste wine, perhaps a very cold and not-too-grand sweet white such as Monbazillac, "country Sauternes."

Much more important than temperature is the question of "weight," or how full bodied a wine is (you can check this by looking at the alcohol content on the label or by swirling it around in a glass and noting now many traces it leaves on the inside of the glass). Even though you can enjoy all sorts of different flavors interleaved—a mouthful of poached halibut followed by one of youthful Claret can be lovely—mixing different weights of food and wine is usually a waste of the "lighter" one. A light cucumber cream mousse would be overwhelmed by a wine as strong as a Hermitage or Barolo, just as a delicate Mosel would be overpowered by the richness of osso buco. With subtly flavored food it makes sense to serve a wine that is not too full bodied. With strongly flavored food, you would be

WITH RICH DESSERTS YOU NEED A VERY SWEET WINE.

foolish to expect a light wine to give much more pleasure than a glass of water. Examples of wines that are particularly light and full bodied are given on page 32. Foods that are very "full" and rich include curries, casseroles, game, and strongly sauced meats; strong cheeses, especially blue ones; rich meat patés, foie gras, and terrines; and smoked fish.

With these guidelines, you should be able to come up with some delicious combinations of food and wine. If it's a casual meal, then your choice of wine may be dictated by which bottle happens to be open—in which case you might well learn all sorts of interesting things about unusual combinations of food and wine.

If you are trying to plan a selection of wines for formal entertaining, however, or simply to maximize informal enjoyment, it is worth bearing in mind the basics of choosing an order for wines:

- **dry before sweet**
- **light before full**
- **young before old**

Remember that four or more of you are likely to open at least a couple of bottles. It can be great fun, and very instructive, to serve two different but related wines at the same time. This has the disadvantage of extra dish washing, and possible accusations of pretension from your guests, but everyone will be surprised by how different two wines can seem when they are tasted together.

You can always take a geographical lead for your choice of wine from what is being cooked. With pasta try an inexpensive Italian, or a better-quality Chianti. Saucisson suggests Beaujolais. A juicy steak could provide an excuse for a stunning Argentine red, while a feta salad or kebabs allow you to introduce your friends to some of the better Greek wines. None of these is expensive. And if you do feel honor bound or perhaps promotion bound (when entertaining the boss) to spend a bit of money for a special dinner, don't splash out on a wine that is not yet ready to drink. Trust your nearest "serious" wine merchant. You can judge how serious they are by the length of their replies to your questions, and they should be delighted to advise on something more exciting than the price of the cheapest quarter bottle of Scotch.

Here's some you might not have thought of
Some more unusual, but still tried-and-tested combinations of food and wine.

Fruity German white with charcuterie
The combination of fairly sweet, light white wine with something as strongly flavored as salami and ham may sound strange, but the wine performs much the same function as a ripe melon with Parma ham, pineapple with gammon, or chutney with baked ham. The principle is that sweetness and saltiness complement each other.

Madeira with clear soup
A dry madeira—Sercial or Verdelho—can be beautifully "nutty" with a meat= or fish-based consommé or an even richer soup.

Smoked salmon and Alsace Riesling or Gewürztraminer
The powerful flavor of any smoked food calls for powerful wine. Riesling is likely to be more elegant.

Foie gras and sweet wine
Sounds disgusting, doesn't it? In fact, any rich livery mousse is delicious with an unctuous sweet wine (it must be fairly full bodied, which rules out most Germans but not the Loire), provided there is a lot of acidity.

Steak or roast meat with a tannic young red or a complex old one
In the case of the young wine, it is the chewiness of the food which distracts from the chewiness of the young wine, making it seem mellower. With very complex old wines, it is a good idea to serve fairly neutral-flavored food without too many distracting accompaniments (and preferably not mint sauce!).

Roast turkey and all seasonal trimmings with Pinot Noir
Roast turkey is, if anything, light on flavor, but those trimmings tend to be so sweet that they can make a Cabernet-based wine seem positively austere. The solution in my view is to serve a quite positively fruity wine that complements this sweetness. Zinfandel is the traditional choice for Thanksgiving dinners, and can work, although the high strength of many of them may rule them out for extended drinking. I think the more delicate Pinot Noir grape is more likely to provide the perfect partner. A fine, not too ambitious Pinot Noir or red Burgundy can be charming, celebratory, fruity, and even slightly sweet-tasting.

Blue cheese and Sauternes

Another strange-sounding combination that works very well, based on much the same salt/sweet principle. Cheese and wine are commonly accepted as ideal partners, and are honored to the extent of having a social function named after them. We naturally enough tend to think that French cheese will be an ideal match for French wine. But next time you have a ripe Camembert or Brie in the house, try it with a mouthful of wine and just see how the ammoniac quality in the cheese wars with the flavor of the wine—making it taste bitter, too. This does not apply to soft fat French cheeses in their youth, nor to the much harder, more cheddarlike Cantal, but certainly to many strong-flavored French fromages—not to mention formaggi such as Gorgonzola. England, so berated by most gastronomes, produces cheeses that are perfect partners for wine. Good farmhouse cheddar is surely the most marvelous accompaniment to all but the most delicate wines; it is firm and offers no strong competition to the flavor of the wine, but still has its own character. Stilton is a bit more difficult. It can be so powerful, and so salty that, like Roquefort, it calls for something very sweet and strong. Port makes sense in the circumstance and proves that I am not trying to be iconoclastic, merely sensible.

Chocolate and Australian Muscat or ruby port

The sweet course is generally served after the cheese in wine-besotted households because cheese, like the main course, can partner dry wines, whereas anything sweet demands a change of gear to a wine that is even sweeter than the food. If that food is very sweet, and there are few desserts sweeter than chocolate-based ones, then the wine also has to be very sweet indeed and, since the flavor of good chocolate is strong, it will also have to be strong in alcohol. An uncomplicated, exuberant young fruity port would be great, as would the even sweeter tawny-colored fortified Black Muscats of northeast Victoria in Australia.

Always remember that, in matters of gastronomy, no matter how hard some people may aspire, there are no ultimate rules or arbiters. No one can point a finger at you and say, "Thou hast sinned by serving me a Mâcon Blanc with hamburger!" If you don't enjoy it, you have only yourself to blame, but your guests should be far too grateful that someone else is taking the trouble to give them a meal to criticize.

Some useful words for wine tasters

I would not call this the definitive wine taster's vocabulary, for such a thing does not exist. The descriptive terms included here are just some of the words you may find helpful to describe sensations caused by wine. Some, indeed most, of these words are quite commonly accepted. Others (marked*) are, quite frankly, humble but mine own. "Blackcurrants" is, for instance, a far-from-unusual description of the Cabernet Sauvignon aroma, but I haven't heard anyone else call the ripe Chenin Blanc of the middle Loire "gummy." Evolve your own vocabulary if it helps you, though a wide range of possible terms has been included here in the hope that specific flavors may lead you to specific grape varieties. Also included is some of the most abstruse jargon, just so you can hold your own in vinous conversation.

acetic a wine gone vinegary by overexposure to air.

acid a wine described as "acid" will have too much acidity.

acidity vital component in wine that gives "bite" and life.

aftertaste strictly the flavor(s) left after the wine is swallowed or spat out, although it is often used interchangeably with finish.

appellation name of the (usually French) designated zone in which the wine was grown. Appellation Contrôlée wines are France's top ones, now representing over 40 percent of production and usually named after the place they were made.

appley some young Chardonnays smell like this, though the smell of unripe apples signals an excess of malic acidity.

aroma the part of the smell of a wine that comes straight from the grapes (c.f. bouquet).

aromatic very strongly perfumed, e.g. Sauvignon and Riesling grape varieties.

astringent the tactile sensation that an excess of tannin leaves on the insides of the mouth. Used especially for white wines (tannic being more generally used for reds).

attenuated smart-sounding term for a wine that is drying out, i.e. losing fruit and charm because of age.

aura* my own word for the "personal bouquet" surrounding the bodies of each of us.

baked a smell of heat and, usually, high alcohol. The flavor is often, but not necessarily, cooked out.

balance vital relative measuring of different elements in a wine, especially sweetness, acidity, fruit, tannin and alcohol. Any good mature wine should be well balanced, though a youthful one may still be "out of balance" because it still has an excess of tannins (in red wine) or acids (in white).

beefy* lots of body and quite a bit of tannin as well.

berries* warm berries veering to berry jam is the giveaway smell of Zinfandel.

blackcurrants aroma of Cabernet Sauvignon, called *cassis* in French. The related Sauvignon Blanc can smell of blackcurrant leaves.

blind tasting an attempt to identify and/or assess wines without knowing their identity. It is the bottles that are masked, not the humans.

blowsy a wine that has a lot of flavor at first, especially on the nose, but has no length and few indications (tannin if red, and acid if white) that it will keep. Almost too much fruit.

body important measure of a wine's weight that is determined chiefly by its alcoholic strength but also by its extract. The more body a wine has the less like water it tastes.

boiled beetroot some people smell this on Pinot Noir.

botrytis cinerea a sort of rot that attacks grapes, shrivelling them and—if they are sweet and white—concentrating their lusciousness to good, and sometimes wonderful, effect. Red wines lose color and are ruined if attacked by this mold, variously known as noble rot, pourriture noble, and Edelfäule.

bottle age the mellowing effect of years spent inside a bottle.

bouquet the smell that derives from fermentation and, most importantly, maturation in bottle (c.f. **aroma**).

breathe (v.i.) what a wine is supposed to do if you leave the bottle open for a bit before serving. This at least gives time for off-flavors (nowadays very uncommon) to dissipate, but the interface between the wine and air is so small (the bottleneck) that this can make little difference. If the wine needs aeration (because it is so young and taut, for instance) slosh it into a decanter or jug.

brett (anomyces) bacteria that live in dirty wooden barrels and can infect wine with an unclean, mousey flavor. A fault to which some American tasters are particularly sensitive, although some producers there associate it so strongly with fine French wine that they deliberately encourage a small amount of brettanomyces.

burnt rubber* smell I associate with the Syrah grape.

buttery the sort of richness (and color) acquired by mature Chardonnay, traditionally associated with Meursault.

carbonic maceration way of making red wine by fermenting the uncrushed grapes. Tends to make full-flavored, deep-colored, low-tannin wines.

cardboard* my term for the smell of stale materials that comes from poor treatment, often overused filter pads.

cats' pee there is something of this in both Sauvignon Blanc and the intensely **aromatic** Scheurebe.

cedarwood the traditional smell of a red Bordeaux given rigorous oak maturation; special characteristic of St. Julien.

chaptalization commonplace (especially in France) practice of adding sugar to grape must to make the resultant wine stronger (though not sweeter).

château literally "castle," but often the name for much less grand wine properties, especially in Bordeaux.

chewy with noticeable **tannins**.

chocolatey* a flavor I find in the often rather **sweet** reds of Australia and especially South Africa.

cigar box synonymous with **cedarwood**.

claret what we British call the red wines of Bordeaux, often labeled Château Something.

classed growth one of the sixty or so châteaux arranged in 1855 into the top five classes from the Médoc and Graves, or included in subsequent classifications of other Bordeaux regions. *Cru classé* is the French term.

clean no off-flavors or nasty smells.

clone particular groups of vines produced from one cutting. Usually chosen in "clonal selection," for one particular attribute such as high yield, disease resistance, or even, praise be, high quality.

closed not very smelly, assumed because of its stage of **maturity**. Similar to **dumb**.

cloying too sweet for the **acidity**.

coarse rough and ordinary, without much interest.

commune French equivalent of a village or parish. Lots of wines are called after the commune in which they were made. A Gevrey-Chambertin is a commune or village wine, for instance, as opposed to one carrying a specific vineyard designation.

complex lots of different, well-married flavors that make a wine interesting, to the point of being fascinating.

concentrated lots of fruit, flavor and, often, color too.

corked/corky wine with a definitely disgusting aroma, mold, or rot. The guilty compound in a corked/corky wine is trichloroanisole (TCA) and is most usually, though not always, caused by a tainted cork. If you smell this particular odor in a restaurant you should send back the wine and ask for another bottle (which is most unlikely to be similarly tainted).

crisp a complimentary term for a white wine with refreshing acidity.

cru literally "growth." A *cru classé* is a classed growth, while a *grand cru* is a great growth.

cuvaison the extra period wine is left on the skins after fermentation to extract more from them.

damp straw* my trigger expression for Chenin Blanc, though many others prefer honey and flowers.

delicate rather airy-fairy term meaning light bodied and without very strong flavor, but well balanced.

dried out old wine in which the initial fruit has faded leaving a deficit of flavor and extract and, sometimes, an apparent excess of acidity.

dumb very little nose, common in good but youthful wine.

Edelfäule see botrytis cinerea.

eucalyptus cough linctus smell common in some concentrated California and Australian Cabernet Sauvignons.

extract important dimension of a wine, the sum of its solids, including tannins, pigments, sugars, minerals, and glycerol.

farmyard* smell I associate with Chianti, especially aged Chianti, with some mature St. Emilion and the odd rustically made Châteauneuf-du-Pape.

fermentation the vital process of turning grape juice into wine is the primary or alcoholic fermentation. The secondary fermentation, encouraged in cellars far from the Equator, is the malo-lactic fermentation that converts harsh malic acid into softer lactic acid.

figs another of those smells that other tasters associate with Sémillon.

finish important part of a wine's impact on the senses, the impression it leaves at the end of the tasting process. A wine with a poor finish fades away to nothingness, and has no length.

firm not flabby, i.e. with sufficient acidity, and not in danger of falling apart because of age or acetic danger.

flabby too low in acidity.

flat dull and boring flavor often without enough acidity, or not sparkling if it is meant to be.

flavor effectively the aroma in the narrowest sense, although some people use flavor to denote the entire impact of a wine on the senses.

flinty confusing but oft-used term usually meaning crisp with a certain suggestion of minerals. Sauvignon Blancs are often called "flinty."

flowery very fragrant in the way that flowers can be; floral scents.

forward a wine is described as forward if it tastes more mature than one would expect for its age.

fresh appealing because of its youth and acidity.

fruit very important component in wines, especially young ones, deriving from the grapes themselves.

fruitcake* how the Merlot grape, especially in St. Emilion, strikes me.

fruity wine with lots of appealing, sometimes sweet **fruit**.

full bodied wine with lots of **body** as opposed to one that is medium bodied or light.

gamey wines that smell pungent in a ripe animal sense, such as a rich Syrah, Mourvèdre, and Merlot (especially Pomerol).

geraniums unpleasant chemical smell, often associated with too much sorbic acid additive.

glycerol colorless, sweet-tasting substance that can add to the impression of **body**.

golden syrup* the smell I associate with rich **sweet** whites, especially those affected by **botrytis**, and particularly Rieslings.

gooseberries "green" sort of smell associated with Sauvignon Blanc, especially the New Zealand sort.

grapey wine that smells of grapes, usually a Muscat.

grassy much as **herbaceous**, though more likely to be used for white wines.

green young wine with too much **acidity**.

guava smell of cool-fermented South African Chenin Blanc.

gummy* the richness that very ripe Chenin Blanc grapes can bring.

gunshot* smell of rich mature Merlot, especially Pomerol. (Just one step ahead of **gamey**, after all.)

hard wine with too much **tannin**.

harmonious well **balanced**.

heavy too much alcohol and too little **acidity** for the **fruit** and sugar levels.

herbaceous smell of grass and leaves, often found in the Cabernet family wines, especially Cabernet Franc.

herby* smell of thyme, lavender, and pine sometimes found (perhaps fancifully) in the Grenache wines of Provence and the Midi.

hock German wines grown on the (sometimes outlying) banks of the Rhine. Wines from such regions come in tallish brown bottles as opposed to the green-bottled Mosel wines.

hollow wine with quite a bit of alcohol, but not much **fruit** to give a satisfying **flavor** and **weight** once in the mouth.

honey (and flowers) traditionally evocative tasting note for Chenin Blanc Loire wines and some German Rieslings.

horizontal tasting a comparative tasting of different but related representatives of the same vintage.

hot too alcoholic.

inky red wine that tastes metallic, **acid**, and often rather **thin**.

juicyfruit* luscious gulpable **fruitiness**, characteristic of Beaujolais.

lanolin rich, almost lemony flavor and texture that is taken on by good-quality Sauternes.

lean lacking **fruit** but not **acid**.

legs the colorless streams left on the inside of a wine glass after a relatively alcoholic wine, more than 12 percent, has been swirled. Often erroneously thought to be **glycerol**, they are sometimes called tears.

length of flavor a giveaway of quality in a wine. Any well-made wine that has had time to mature should leave a long aftertaste once it has been swallowed or expectorated. It "finishes well."

licorice some people smell this in mature Nebbiolo, others in some red Burgundies.

lift(ed) wine with a perceptible but not excessive level of volatility.

light the opposite of **full bodied** and not a pejorative term for wines that are meant to be delicate, such as many dry whites and some reds destined for youthful consumption.

lively a wine that seems bursting with **fruit** and **flavor**; often due to a very slight "prickle" of carbon dioxide in the wine, which may for this reason be left intentionally by its maker.

long a wine with good **length**, or a good **finish**, is long.

maderized sometimes used instead of **oxidized** for a white wine, especially when it is meant without malice—e.g. for a fortified wine such as madeira (from which the name derives) or for a very old wine that is still interesting despite slight oxidation.

maturity that period in a wine's development after its youth and before it starts to decline. It can be after three years or after three decades, depending on the wine. "Mature" is a complimentary term, as opposed to "old" or "faded," which are criticisms.

meaty substantial and **full bodied** in **flavor**, often just as the **tannin** is starting to reveal the **fruit**.

mellow sometimes used by red wine marketeers as a euphemism for **sweet**.

mercaptan substance formed by hydrogen sulphide (H_2S) that smells like rotten eggs. A fault in wine, and one to which Australians are particularly sensitive.

middle palate jargon for what we sense between the initial impact of a wine in the mouth and the **finish**, as in "there is not much **fruit** on the middle palate."

minerally* smell of assorted minerals and a common component of fine Cabernet and Riesling.

minty many people smell this spearmint (not peppermint) flavor in California Cabernets, especially those from the Napa Valley.

Mosel German wine in tallish green bottles, produced in the valley of the Mosel (Moselle in France).

mousey nasty smell associated with **brettanomyces**, a bacteriological fault.

mouthfeel American term for the physical impact of a wine on the mouth, and its texture, heavily influenced by both **tannin** and **body**.

mulberries* smell (and color) I associate with Syrah.

must grape pulp mixture that ferments into wine.

noble adjective used to describe those grape varieties that are most respected and that can produce wines that mature to magnificence. Cabernet Sauvignon, Merlot, Pinot Noir, Syrah, Nebbiolo, Chardonnay, Riesling, and Sémillon are the most obvious candidates, but almost all of the grape varieties mentioned in this book apart from Trebbiano and Colombard have some claim to nobility—and there are bottles that prove that even these have some blue blood.

noble rot see **botrytis cinerea**.

nose (v.t. and n.) the nose of a wine is its **bouquet** or **aroma**, depending on its state of **maturity**. It is the **flavor** you can smell. You nose a wine when you consciously smell it.

oaky a wine that smells and tastes of oak, a good or a bad thing depending on whether you like it (c.f. **woody**).

oxidized wine that has been exposed to air and as a result has become stale and flat.

peachy* self-explanatory smell I associate with Viognier.

pear drops rather chemical smell reminiscent of acetate or nail-polish remover, sometimes found in youthful Beaujolais.

pencil shavings* the smell (of the wood not the lead) I find in Cabernet Franc.

perfumed wine with lots of smellable flavor, usually of a slightly musky sort. A white wine adjective.

petillant slightly sparkling, same as spritz(ig).

petit château wine from a single Bordeaux property that is not officially classified, i.e. not a *cru classé*.

petrol flavor of mature Riesling, especially German.

plummy rich fruitiness particularly associated with mature Merlot.

pourriture noble French for botrytis cinerea.

powerful lots of very easy-to-perceive flavor, plus alcohol.

pricked same as acetic.

prickle slight sparkle, same as spritz(ig).

racy lively, used often for white wine, especially Riesling.

raspberries characteristic scent of Pinot Noir. Some find that Zinfandel smells of raspberries, too.

residual sweetness amount of sweetness left in the wine after fermentation has been completed.

rich luscious and full bodied, though not necessarily very sweet. A rich red wine may taste slightly sweet (not a word often used to describe reds) but probably because of its alcohol content.

rotten eggs smell of mercaptan or hydrogen sulphide (H_2S).

round good body, not too much tannin.

short wine with no length of flavor.

smoky characteristic of many Alsace whites and the Chardonnay grape; a broad sort of flavor.

soft wine with too little tannin, so applicable to red wine only.

soupy wine with no distinct flavor, usually low in acidity and quite full bodied.

sparkling in Europe, where the lawyers of Champagne have influence, all wine that fizzes, but is not made in the Champagne region, is called sparkling wine.

spicy Gewürztraminer has an exotic floral or lychee sort of "spice," while some red grapes, notably Merlot, have a fruity sort.

spritz(ig) slightly sparkling wines.

steely rather loose term used chiefly for whites such as Sauvignon and very cool-climate Chardonnays, meaning they have lots of acidity and a very pure flavor.

still not sparkling.

sulfury wines that have an excess of the much-used winemaker's disinfectant sulfur dioxide (SO_2) may smell of recently struck matches or coke-fired ovens. The smell can be dissipated by swirling the offending wine around the glass.

supple wine without too much tannin and lots of attractive fruit, usually applied to fairly youthful reds in which one might not expect such a quality, e.g. Cabernets.

sweet self-explanatory, but rarely used for red wines.

tannic wine containing lots of tannin.

tannin preservative that comes from the skins, stalks, and pips of grapes (and from wood, too) which tastes like cold stewed tea.

tar some people smell this on Nebbiolo wines, others on Syrah. Both grapes have a depth of color that helps the auto-suggestion along.

tart wine with too much youthful **acidity**. A pejorative term similar to **green**.

thin wine lacking **body**, to the extent of being watery.

tobacco leaves* flavor I associate with Tempranillo (different from cigars and **cigar boxes**).

trigger word* expression used to trigger a mental impression of a wine. If I smell Tempranillo, for instance, I say "tobacco" to myself and can therefore identify it as such. Very useful for **blind tasting**, and for measuring samples against the acceptable norm.

truffles some tasters find this elusive scent in the Nebbiolo wines of Piedmont, great white truffle country.

vanilla self-explanatory flavor closely associated with American oak, in which almost all red Rioja and many California reds are matured.

vapor* my term for the **volatiles** a wine gives off to communicate its **flavor** to your olfactory receptors, and thence to the brain.

varietal varietal wine (American term) is named after the predominant grape variety from which it was made. This is in contrast to generic wines, named after a wine region and, supposedly, style. Thus there used to be in Britain, and still are in America and Australia, wines labeled Burgundy, Claret, and even Sauterne (no "s" on the end) because they are made (dimly) in the reflection of those regions' style.

vegetal wine smelling of assorted vegetative matter. Not quite reminiscent of the hedgerow, as **herbaceous** is, but of the vegetable patch. Pinot Noir often has this flavor.

velvety description of texture, usually used for wines with lots of glycerine and not much **tannin**.

vertical tasting a comparative tasting of different vintages from the same provenance.

vinegary smelling **acetic**.

vintage either the harvest or the year of the harvest.

violets smell some associate with Nebbiolo, others with Pinot Noir.

vitis vinifera the European family of vines whose grapes are particularly suitable for making wine, as opposed to most other vine families, many of which are American in origin.

volatile something that is volatile vaporizes easily and gives off lots of volatiles that comprise what I have called a wine's **vapor**, which conveys the **flavor** of a wine to the olfactory receptors. All wines are volatile to a greater or lesser extent. The warmer they are and the more **aromatic** the grape varieties from which they were made, the more volatile they will be. A wine is described as volatile if it is in fact too volatile, i.e. it is giving off flavor so readily that it starts to taste **acetic**.

weedy* a combination of **herbaceous** and **tart**.

weight all wines have one and, just as for people, it's a measure of how much **body** they have.

woody the unacceptable face of oak: a nasty, wet, moldy sort of flavor that comes (but not often) from a cask in poor condition.

yeasty smell of fermenting yeasts.

yield the amount of wine produced per area of vines. The French measure it in hectolitres per hectare and call it *rendement*. Thirty is low and one hundred high.

index

acknowledgments

The publisher would like to thank the following photographers and organizations for their kind permission to reproduce the photographs in this book.

14 Steve Elphick/Cephas; 24 John Miller/Robert Harding Picture Library; 25 Jan Traylen/Patrick Eagar Photography; 28 & 35 Mick Rock/Cephas; 37 Diana Mewes/Cephas; 42 Robert Harding Picture Library; 46 Diana Mewes/Cephas; 57 Geoff Lung/Vogue Entertaining; 58 Simon Shepheard/IMPACT; 63 Nick Dolding/Tony Stone Images; 68 Patrick Eagar Photography; 72, 84 & 88 Mick Rock/Cephas; 91 Patrick Eagar Photography; 95 Adrian Lander; 99 Mick Rock/Cephas; 101 Robert Harding Picture Library; 102 Mick Rock/Cephas; 106 Kevin Judd/Cephas; 109 Patrick Eagar Photography; 111, 113, 116, 120, 123 & 124 Mick Rock/Cephas; 126 Melanie Acevedo; 129 Mick Rock/Cephas; 132 R & K Muschenetz/Cephas; 134 Mick Rock/Cephas; 136 Andy Christodolo/Cephas; 139 Mick Rock/Cephas; 140 Patrick Eagar Photography; 142 Kevin Judd/Cephas; 144 & 146 Mick Rock/Cephas; 149 David Martyn Huges/Robert Harding Picture Library; 150 Mick Rock/Cephas; 152 Michael Busselle; 153 Patrick Eagar Photography; 157 Mick Rock/Cephas; 159 Michael Short/Robert Harding Picture Library; 161 Lucy Davies/Axiom Photographic Agency; 162 C Bowman/Robert Harding Picture Library; 164 Ted Stefanski/Cephas; 171 Mick Rock/Cephas; 175 Patrick Eagar Photography; 177 Michael Busselle; 181 Mick Rock/Cephas; 182 Michael Jenner/Robert Harding Picture Library; 186 Hotze Eisma/Taverne Agency; 188 Tom Odulate/Camera Press; 192 Mick Rock/Cephas; 194 Alexander van Berge

Every effort has been made to trace the copyright holders and we apologize in advance for any unintentional omission and would be pleased to insert the appropriate acknowledgment in any subsequent edition.

The publisher and author would also like to thank Cantina Vinopolis (020 7940 8333) for their help and cooperation in our location photography. Thanks also to Howard G. Goldberg for his valuable contribution to the American edition of this book.